TIME-TESTED

The Stoic Negotiator's Five Keys
for the Modern Deal

Douglas J. Witten

Innovative ADR International LLC

Copyright © 2024 Innovative ADR International LLC

All rights reserved

The characters and events portrayed in this book are fictitious. Any similarity to real persons, living or dead, is coincidental and not intended by the author.

No part of this book may be reproduced, or stored in a retrieval system, or transmitted in any form or by any means, electronic, mechanical, photocopying, recording, or otherwise, without express written permission of the publisher.

ISBN-13:
ISBN-10:

Cover design by: Josh Murphy
Library of Congress Control Number:
Printed in the United States of America

You always own the option of having no opinion. There is never any need to get worked up or to trouble your soul about things you can't control. These things are not asking to be judged by you. Leave them alone.

MARCUS AURELIUS

CONTENTS

Title Page
Copyright
Epigraph
INTRODUCTION
STOICISM: LAYING THE FOUNDATION — 1
FIVE KEY PRINCIPLES — 11
PRINCIPLE ONE: EMOTIONS — 14
PRINCIPLE TWO: CONTROL — 57
PRINCIPLE THREE: OBJECTIVITY — 82
PRINCIPLE FOUR: HUMILITY — 111
PRINCIPLE FIVE: EMPATHY — 138
About The Author — 159
Books By This Author — 161

INTRODUCTION

Michael walked away from $500,000 – more money than he'd ever seen in his life – and he would've never known it.

Why? Because he lost control of negotiations at the worst possible moment.

This middle-aged gentleman, Michael, had been working with his attorney in efforts to settle a difficult lawsuit he brought against a former employer. After having this dispute hang over his head for years, Michael and his counsel finally had an opportunity to resolve the case.

Months of negotiation had culminated in an 8-hour settlement mediation conference. On this particular day, I was brought in as a mediator – a neutral, independent professional specializing in helping parties negotiate – to assist Michael and his ex-employer resolve their differences amicably. A negotiated agreement would mean a monetary settlement for Michael and a closed case for his ex-employer.

The Backdrop

Mediation is a highly useful process that offers a number of advantages over traditional courtroom litigation. It's basically a structured, guided negotiation.

Besides the benefits of speed, efficiency, low cost, and self-determination (*i.e.*, you control your fate), among others, mediation gives the parties a chance to collaborate and settle their disputes without having to go to trial. If nothing else, mediation allows litigants to take matters into their own hands instead of rolling the proverbial dice before a judge and jury.

Michael and his lawyer had struggled at times throughout his mediation, as the case was complex and gave them much to consider, and they finally had the finish line in sight.

That's when everything fell apart for Michael.

As we approached the eighth hour of mediation negotiations, gathered in an office conference space, the defendant ex-employer was on the verge of extending their top offer. Following an initial joint meeting among the parties and their lawyers, we'd been working most of the day in separate, private mediation caucus rooms.

I had just finished an honest, deep conversation with the defense room. Although they didn't agree with Michael's assessment of his case, they understood why his lawyer and he felt as they did. The defense team realized that reasonable minds could differ on the facts and law surrounding the case and, thus, monetary settlement ranges. Michael and his attorney had actually succeeded in communicating their perspectives to the former employer, and the defense team acknowledged that they'd learned new information and re-thought their position throughout the day.

So that was good. We were making progress.

Check Yourself

Just as the tide was shifting in the defense room, unbeknownst to me, things were coming off the rails for Michael. I left the defense as they continued crunching numbers. Meanwhile, I knocked on Michael's team's conference room door and then entered.

"So . . . little change in plans here. My client . . . uh, Michael . . . he just left. I begged him not to, but he wouldn't listen. I don't know what else to do."

Michael's attorney's words hung in the air for a moment as I digested them and considered how to respond. I knew her client was somewhat tense and had been challenged throughout the day's proceedings. Still, this blindsided me as I entered the vacated caucus room.

"Huh?!? You've gotta be kidding me," was my first insight.

No, no one was kidding. And then we started to unpack the situation.

"My client just lost it," Michael's attorney explained. "He hid it from you so well. But the other side's negotiation tactics were making him madder, and madder, until he completely blew his cool and went home."

"So, without telling me or the other side, he got up and left, after all of this?" I asked, incredulously. "And why didn't we talk about the approaching boiling point during our private caucus meetings?"

How Do You Value a Missed Opportunity?

The end result was that Michael and his lawyer never made it to the end of the mediation. Apparently, in a flash of anger, despair, and impatience, Michael lost his composure. He verbally lashed out at his own lawyer and supporting family members, and he then proceeded to exit the building.

Despite the encouragement of everyone on his team, Michael lapsed in focus during a process that requires your "A" game to optimize results. On this day, Michael was hung up on the past and couldn't see his case from all sides. He had been living with his lawsuit for so long that he was angry and driven by revenge. The defense's negotiating approach hadn't been ideal. Yet Michael was not even willing to consider what the other side was saying. He certainly didn't care about his ex-employer's motivations or inability to offer what he demanded.

Michael had every right to feel the way he did. No one else stands in his shoes, and Michael makes his own negotiation decisions. As a mediator, I don't decide case results or tell people what to think or feel. Michael's lawyer can advise him to a point, but ultimately Michael is in charge. I did all I could to help both sides reach an agreement that day, but Michael simply wasn't hearing it.

So after nearly eight hours, I understood Michael's frustration. Still, I was certain there remained a mutual opportunity for the parties to reach a resolution.

"Yep. This is devastating. The worst part is," counsel continued, "we had room to negotiate. Significantly more room. And we could've resolved this lawsuit, once and for all."

The Cost of Ongoing Conflict

In Michael's case, I knew failure to settle meant the parties' risking a chance to save themselves significant time, money, and potential risk. Going to trial is uncertain, often expensive and drawn out, and you cede control of the outcome to a judge and jury. Consensual negotiation, on the other hand, allows parties to regain autonomy and resolve their disputes amicably and efficiently.

The mediation process works best when the parties at least uncover their best options. When parties give up prematurely – whether due to impatience, misdirected emotional responses, lack of negotiating skill, or any other non-substantive reason – they are missing potential opportunities. If you don't know what the other party is ultimately willing to offer, or accept, to resolve a case or resolve a dispute, how can you possibly make an educated decision?

Unfortunately, on this day, Michael squandered his moment. And it had nothing to do with the underlying substance of the negotiation – despite their differing positions, the parties' case evaluations weren't that far apart. Instead, Michael lost his chance because he let his emotions get the best of him and, with that, committed the cardinal sin of negotiation.

Michael's mediation is one that has stuck with me over the ensuing years. As a professional mediator, I'm used to conflict. I know that lawsuits can be highly upsetting, emotional events, and negotiating towards resolution of these cases can be very stressful.

Mediators are trained to view disputes dispassionately and objectively, and help parties "see the forest for the trees." But this task can be challenging. And even for a mediator, a neutral party with no stake in the outcome of a negotiation, cases like Michael's are tough to shake.

Michael's case epitomized how so much of dispute resolution and negotiation success goes beyond the substance of a conflict.

Master the Process, Manage the Result . . . Every Day

That is, Michael and his ex-employer had joint interest in settling this case. It was to their mutual benefit to resolve the dispute quickly, efficiently, and amicably. Furthermore, despite their differing positions on the facts and law entering negotiations, the parties' respective settlement ranges left them a tremendous opportunity to compromise.

But they didn't negotiate well. Even with the assistance of a neutral mediator – a luxury not all parties to a dispute will have – the two sides weren't connecting. No, not every case is meant to be settled, and sometimes going to court is the only viable option. Here, though, the tragedy occurs when the parties give up on negotiating before they even know what they're walking away from.

The more I thought about his case, too, the more I realized that *we replicate Michael's missteps in everyday conflicts and negotiations all the time*.

It's usually on a smaller scale and with lower stakes involved, of course. Still, we can all relate to Michael's most unfortunate – and human – negotiation failings. Thus, we can also learn from them.

Consider for yourself:

How many times do we allow our emotions to get the better of us during a heated discussion?

When in conflict situations, do we become frustrated or distracted by things over which we have no control?

How often do we find ourselves in arguments in which our counterparts don't appreciate our side of the issue but, instead, are sure they have all the answers?

And when was the last time we really, truly tried to put ourselves in the shoes of our adversaries and figure out why they view things so differently?

As you ponder these questions and the broader implications of Michael's negotiation miscues, let's take a quick look at what went wrong and why it matters.

Opportunities Lost

As a negotiator, Michael, in sum, failed at a critical time to:

(1) manage his **emotions**;
(2) focus on what he could **control**;
(3) seek out **objectivity**;
(4) approach with **humility**; and
(5) lead with **empathy**.

Remember these key points, as we'll be later be delving into them. Meanwhile, think about a negotiation situation in which you might've succumbed to any or all of these failings. How did that impact your results?

For now, let me share some good news. Michael's story actually has a fortunate ending.

Although mediation-day negotiations went down in a blaze, I was later able to help the parties and their attorneys steer discussions back on track. Over a period of about 3 weeks after Michael's mediation, I reached out to both sides multiple times and ultimately shepherded their negotiations across the finish line.

In the end, the employer was willing to offer an amount squarely within Michael's target settlement range. Don't get me wrong – the two sides never agreed on every element of the case or wholeheartedly on the case's value. Nonetheless, we were able to restore Michael's comfort with the negotiation process and break through the "noise" that was distorting both sides' viewpoints. Only then, the parties saw clearly that their interests in resolution overlapped enough to let them settle the case.

News You Can Use

There's good news from Michael's case for the rest of us, too. Michael's tale reminds us that although in some respects all negotiations are unique, in other ways they share common elements and pitfalls. After working with thousands of parties in mediation settings over the years, I've had front row seats for many spectacular triumphs and, unfortunately, a few tragic negotiation failures.

Looking back, I'm still amazed that Michael concealed his frustration from me so well during the mediation. (I'm even more amazed that his attorney didn't advise me of what she should have perceived as an enormous problem, but that's another matter.) Given the opportunity to help on the front end, I'm confident we could've mitigated the situation on the spot.

Regardless, though Michael's negotiations were noteworthy in that they unraveled so quickly, Michael's reactions and resulting errors felt familiar. In fact, knowing how people might be tempted to respond in the heat of the moment, I often share some version of these suggestions to mediation participants feeling negotiation pressure:

If you haven't expended your best effort at mediation, if you aren't convinced the other side has expended their best effort, or both, then why give up? How can you make a truly reasoned decision otherwise?

Exiting a mediation in a huff might provide you an instant of relief from what you find to be a frustrating situation, but consider the long-term view. Take a break if you need to, talk with your client or counsel or mediator, go for a walk, and clear your head however you can.

Don't send a mediation off the rails because you lack the discipline to dig in and do the hard work. Often, the best chance to strike a deal will arise at mediation, when all parties – at least in theory – will be focused on the dispute and pooling mental, emotional, and economic resources to resolve it amicably.

If you need to reconvene on another date or continue negotiations telephonically, electronically, or by video, when cooler heads prevail, that's fine, too. Keep your mediation session cordial and at the very least have the courtesy to face the other side, inform opposing counsel and the mediator of your intentions, and leave the lines of communication open. Talk to the mediator and rely on his or her skills to help you see the process through to its conclusion.

You always have the ability to turn down an offer and reach a point of impasse; self-determination is a hallmark of the mediation process. Just make sure you know what you're walking away from before you give up on negotiations.

I've been surprised so many times by the twists and turns a mediation can take that I will always be the last one to throw in the proverbial towel. People are predictably unpredictable, so let the mediation process play out to unveil your best prospects for a negotiated agreement.

At the same time, I recognize that – let's face it – conflict, negotiation, and dispute resolution are hard. As a neutral mediator, I have the luxury of being able to remove myself from a dispute's emotional components and view situations from an outsider's 360-degree vantage. When we're embroiled in conflict, though, and we have a personal, financial, emotional, or other stake in the outcome, the challenges mount quickly. This can be true in high-stakes scenarios like Michael's as well as in low-dollar, more run-of-the-mill negotiations.

Finally, the key revelation: Michael's negotiation flop provides us a perfect segue to improving our own everyday negotiation skills. Fortunately, most of our daily conflicts don't involve life-altering lawsuits, years of pent-up frustration towards a former employer, and negotiation decisions featuring hundreds of thousands of dollars hanging in the balance.

However, in conflict and negotiation settings we all face elements of what Michael faced.

Sure, you want to avoid calamitous errors if you ever confront a situation like Michael's. The reality, though, is that your everyday life provides more than ample opportunity to hone your negotiating skills and use them on a regular basis.

The more you can focus on the building blocks of a sound negotiation and conflict-resolution mindset, and the more you strengthen and utilize your dispute-solving tools, the better prepared you'll be. *The better negotiator you'll be.*

Remember those areas where we said Michael came up short? Again, they are: (1) emotions; (2) control; (3) objectivity; (4) humility; and (5) empathy. These are the negotiation building blocks we'll be examining throughout this book.

Michael's negotiation deficiencies nearly cost him a life-changing settlement. You don't want your negotiating capacity *ever* to let you down, even on a smaller stage.

Further still, why not aim higher and *optimize* your everyday negotiations? Considering all of our daily opportunities to negotiate, persuade, and resolve conflicts – basically, whenever we're engaging with someone in hopes that they'll see things differently or act in a certain way – how much better off would you be with winning negotiation skills?

It all starts with having a solid foundation and proper mindset entering negotiations and disputes. For those things, fortunately, you've come to the right place.

So settle in, and let's get to work.

STOICISM: LAYING THE FOUNDATION

In the middle of 2015, I began seriously considering opening my own mediation and arbitration practice. With experience initially as a big-firm corporate attorney and later as a government lawyer, I was struck by inspiration. I was ready to return to the private sector, start my own business, and focus on helping people resolve disputes more effectively as a professional negotiator and arbiter.

I knew I loved mediating and was excited to carve my path as a private dispute-resolver. However, to do that I'd need to make a leap. I would have to leave a comfortable, stable government job, which was fine enough. But I didn't love it. I wasn't passionate about my work, and I wanted to be. I *needed* to be.

Years of preparation and honing my craft had brought me to an inflection point. I had trekked to the edge of the cliff, strapped on my bungee cord, contemplated the gulf below . . . and all that was left was to take the leap.

As I considered my future, during that year and the several preceding, I sought guidance from different sources. I talked with mentors about their career paths. I spoke with family and friends who knew me and could offer insights and advice. Of course, my wife and I discussed work options at length, and how a job change would affect our daily family life. I also performed a ton of research, read all sorts of books, articles, and journals related to starting a practice, and spoke with as many mediators and arbitrators as I could. I even worked with a career coach and a resume consultant, looking anywhere and everywhere for constructive guidance.

At some point during my deliberations, I reconnected with a philosophy that not only would propel me to open my business and forever change my career path, but also continues to shape the way I perform my work, approach life, and exercise the art of mediation.

"How long are you going to wait before you demand the best for yourself?" wrote Epictetus.

That was the quote that struck a chord with me most, the words that gave me the jolt I needed to enter the great unknown. I left the comfort of a familiar job, acknowledged it *was* high time to demand the best for myself, and pursued the career I'd always dreamt about.

In coming across the writings of Epictetus, a Greek philosopher who lived about 2,000 years ago, I also plunged into the world of Stoicism. That's when the seed for this book was first planted.

I had learned a bit about this ancient philosophy in college and graduate school, which provided my first introduction to the Stoics. Since then, the ancient philosophy they created, which has shaped so many men and women throughout history, has immeasurably changed my life.

Quite literally, every single day includes some combination of reading, writing, listening to, and utilizing aspects of Stoicism that creates satisfaction and directly enhances my sense of well-being. This philosophy not only helps me be a more effective negotiator, but also makes me a better person.

After mediating many hundreds of cases at this point in my career – serving as a neutral party, guiding litigants through a consensual negotiation process – I have had the pleasure of helping thousands of parties resolve lawsuits by forging amicable settlements, instead of languishing in an uncertain and inefficient court system for months or years. Over time, it has become more and more clear to me that many of the lessons of Stoicism have direct application in negotiation settings.

The last bit bears repeating, as it sits at the core of this writing: *Critical lessons of Stoicism directly apply in negotiation settings.*

This book explains how.

Stoic Mediator, Stoic Negotiator

I have written this book to share a collection of Stoic-inspired lessons that can help you maximize your potential as negotiators and conflict-resolvers. This is not a history book, and it does not profile the great Stoic philosophers who have lived over the years. Nor is this book designed to wrap you up in hypothetical theories that make your head spin.

Instead, this book should serve as a call to action. It will help you improve your negotiation preparation and execution. And perhaps this book will even inspire you to think completely differently about negotiation, persuasion, and conflict resolution.

Building from lessons inspired by the ancient Stoics, and others reflecting Stoic teachings, I have outlined ways to apply certain bedrock principles directly to negotiation. Absorbing these lessons, and harnessing them in your next formal or informal negotiation setting – or whenever you find yourself in a conflict or dispute – will help you become a better negotiator and reach more satisfactory outcomes.

You could spend a lifetime reading the Stoics, studying the likes of Seneca, Epictetus, Zeno, Marcus Aurelius, Cato, and others. Perhaps you've already begun your journey, or maybe you're now hearing of Stoicism for the first time. So for some this collection might serve as the most brief introduction to Stoic philosophy, and for others it could provide a new twist on beloved principles. Either way, this book gives you a practical guide that shines a light on how a time-tested philosophy can influence and improve your life and work.

A constructive goal of philosophy is to "turn words into works," as renowned Stoic Seneca might say. Stoicism doesn't ask us to sit around and think and ponder. This philosophy is about action, doing, and applying. You can have all the deep thoughts in the world, but if you don't put them into practice, what's the point?

"Don't explain your philosophy. Embody it," noted Epictetus.

This book provides you a selection of negotiation themes and lessons, organized into five guiding principles, inspired by the Stoics. Read them, learn them, and apply them. Use them today, tomorrow, next week, and next year.

The lessons are time-tested and are older than any of us. So let them work for you now.

What is Stoicism? (And who cares, anyway?)

Stoicism is an ancient Greco-Roman branch of philosophy we can draw upon to help become more resilient, virtuous, and wise, better people overall. Generally, the philosophy started with Zeno (a philosopher who lived and taught in Athens around 300 B.C.) over 2,000 years ago. Stoicism became very popular in the West and has in recent years experienced a rediscovery – a renaissance, of sorts – in our popular culture.

Other key early figures include:

- Marcus Aurelius (121-180 CE): most famous Stoic; 2nd Century Roman emperor, author of *Meditations*;
- Epictetus (50-135 CE): former slave-turned-lecturer and teacher; lived in Greece and Rome; known for *The Enchiridion*; and
- Seneca (5 BCE-65 CE): famous Roman playwright and political advisor to Nero; wrote *Letters from a Stoic*, *Discourses*.

Stoicism has influenced leaders and thinkers throughout

history, such as Frederick the Great, George Washington, Thomas Jefferson, Adam Smith, Immanuel Kant, and John Stuart Mill. Interestingly, too, Stoicism has experienced a revival in recent years among athletes, celebrities, and public figures – like Admiral James Stockdale, Arnold Schwarzenegger, Anna Kendrick, Bill Belichick, Brie Larson, LL Cool J, Michele Tafoya, Nick Saban, Pete Carroll, and many more – who have in some way rediscovered the practical wisdom and practices of Stoicism.

Austrian psychotherapist Viktor Frankl's Holocaust memoir, *Man's Search for Meaning*,[1] should be on everyone's essential reading list. Frankl's work is a startling exemplar of how Stoic principles can lead us through even the most agonizing hardships. More recently, popular podcasters and authors like Ryan Holiday, Tim Ferriss, and Sam Harris have helped embed Stoicism firmly in our zeitgeist.

That any philosophy can stand the test of time and guide our lives today, as it did 2,000 years ago, is a credit to its enduring wisdom and relatability. The more things change, the more they stay the same. People are people, and what's old is new again. That's why Stoicism now is as relevant as ever.

Generally speaking, Stoicism is a philosophy that aids in the pursuit of self-mastery, perseverance, and wisdom. It promotes keeping a calm mind, and building strength and stamina for life's challenges.

You can spend a lifetime studying and practicing Stoicism, like most schools of philosophy. But Stoicism also stands out for its practicality and the fact that we can break it down into usable concepts.

Among those key Stoic concepts:

- Your mind creates your reality, and your mind can be trained.

- Fate exists and is beyond our control.

- Events both good and bad will happen in our lives. And our greatest power resides in the moment we choose how to respond.

- Building on the last point: Stoics believe they don't control the world around them, only how they respond. And they must respond with courage, temperance, justice, and wisdom – the 4 Stoic virtues.

- Bad things are going to happen in life; no matter what, we always have the capacity to use reason and make choices. We should always try to do the right thing.

- *Amor fati*. Love your fate, a Stoic would say. Embrace every moment, no matter how challenging it might be, as it could not have been any other way. Make the most of it, and be better because of it.

Stoic ideas influenced cognitive behavioral therapy (CBT) — a popular form of psychotherapy — that teaches patients not to dwell on the past, but to focus on making healthier decisions in the present, thereby creating a better future. The Serenity Prayer, a powerful recitation for so many in addiction treatment, borrows directly from Stoicism, asking for the grace to accept the things one cannot control, as well as the courage to change the things one can.

Why Should Negotiators Explore Stoicism?

I have a confession to make: I'm certainly not a philosopher. I'm a mediator, so I'm working with people stuck in conflict and trying to negotiate their way out to something better. And what's great about Stoicism is that it's practical and relatable. You can put it to use and rely on it every day and, as I've found, we as negotiators can lean on Stoic teachings and incorporate key concepts into our toolkits.

First and foremost, study Stoicism to help you live a good, virtuous life! I was initially attracted to Stoicism because it helps build mental toughness. As a long-distance runner, and also as an attorney and entrepreneur, I was instinctively drawn to it. Ryan Holliday, Tim Ferriss, and others studying habits of high-performers and peak performance have been leading a renewed interest in this philosophy, too.

The more I've studied Stoicism and observed and experienced effective negotiation approaches, I see a lot of overlap. In fact, various Stoic tools and concepts directly lead to improved, real-world, negotiation results.

As we've said, the more things change, the more they stay the same. While there's currently considerable excitement about the use of artificial intelligence (AI) in negotiation – and, as in countless other realms, rightly so – the increasing reliance on technology puts a premium on a negotiator's ability to master the basics of emotion management and controlling ego, for example.

As long as people are involved in conflict and decision-making, the very human skills we can learn from Stoicism give us a leg up. Arguably, as AI proceeds to assist perhaps with more fact-driven and technical disputes and negotiations, the premium on managing emotions and interpersonal relations (and the advantage to those skilled in these areas) – and investing in negotiation and conflict resolution skills – will increase even further.

For negotiators, AI forces us to look in the mirror and ask this essential question:

Which of our negotiation abilities are uniquely human, and how can we master those?

Negotiating Like a Stoic

Effective negotiation approaches that we identify here embody practical application of Stoic principles. That is, this book is about improving your negotiating using time-tested philosophical tools.

Starting from the 4 Stoic virtues of courage, temperance, justice, and wisdom, we can build a framework – a mindset – to rely on when we get into challenging negotiation situations.

My experience negotiating has taught me that managing emotions, seeing things objectively, and reckoning with the outcomes we can control and the uncertainties we can't, are all critical negotiation skills.

Luckily, we have a practical, accessible, 2,000-year-old philosophy that helps guide us in those areas.

Stoicism helps us organize our thoughts, emotions, and behaviors in a manner that promotes tranquility. Stoics turn obstacles into opportunity, as do effective negotiators. Stoics know that there's no good or bad, just perception, and that perception is in your control. Likewise, the skilled negotiator, even under pressure, is able to respond dispassionately and turn challenges into opportunities.

So these concepts in particular are incredibly useful guides during negotiations. When you think about turning hardship into hope, managing egos and perspectives, and staying strong in the face of adversity . . . these are all valuable components of what an effective negotiator must do.

There's a time and place for negotiation "formulas," or sales scripts, or even checklists for negotiation. But the bottom line is that people are all different and formulas can get you into trouble.

Every negotiation is unique, and you can't rely on a single blueprint. You need to be flexible and adaptable to the situations that present themselves, another reason why having a sound foundation is so important. As tempting as it is to seek out shortcuts, tricks, "top ten" lists, and flavor-of-the-month negotiation acronyms, proceed with caution.

Stoicism affords a framework for improvising on the fly and adapting your approach to the particular situation and personalities involved. Guiding principles from the likes of Epictetus, Marcus Aurelius, and Seneca carry a certain weight after a couple of millennia. When it comes to undergirding our conflict resolution skills, then, there is no reason to reinvent the wheel.

This approach is for people who want to see the big picture. Before you can get to strategy and tactics, you must have the foundation. That is what the Stoic philosophy can provide.

At home, at work, in formal negotiation settings involving business deals or legal matters, we're negotiating constantly. Entering conflicts, disagreements, and difficult conversations with the right mental framework is the first step towards developing better negotiation skills and then, ultimately, getting more of what you want in negotiated outcomes.

The Stoic Negotiator™ and YOU!

I've been a professional mediator — helping people negotiate, resolve conflict, and reach agreements — since 2003. I've worked with thousands of parties in dispute and have learned from interacting with so many people and studying their paths to successful negotiation. I've seen a lot of what's effective, and a lot of what isn't, in dealing with different personalities and resolving business disputes.

I'm also a fan of the Stoic philosophy, which has been around for 2,000 years, as by now you've likely gathered. What's motivated me to delve into the intersection of Stoicism and negotiation? I've been surprised — shocked, really — how much the work of these ancient philosophers can teach us about negotiation today.

To that end, towards the close of 2020, I launched *The Stoic Negotiator™* (https://stoicnegotiator.substack.com) periodic newsletter. The newsletter shares practical ideas about how we can become better everyday negotiators, incorporating certain Stoic principles into our daily routines, and negotiate more successfully.

The Stoic Negotiator™ highlights concepts, ideas, mindsets, approaches, and strategies — inspired by Stoic philosophy — that can help us become more effective negotiators and resolvers of conflict.

This book now curates from *The Stoic Negotiator™* a collection of entries you can use to become a better negotiator. Thus, each entry that follows is derived from a newsletter publication delivered to subscribers of *The Stoic Negotiator™*.

As you'll see, the book's organization centers upon the five negotiation building blocks we referenced earlier: (1) emotions; (2) control; (3) objectivity; (4) humility; and (5) empathy. For each of these principles, inspired by the Stoics, representative book chapters illustrate the point through a general explanation bolstered by practical negotiation examples.

FIVE KEY PRINCIPLES

s a reminder and overview, let's summarize quickly our five negotiation building blocks:

1. Emotions: Managing, regulating, and channeling emotion is a principal theme familiar to any student of Stoicism. And that theme is common among skilled negotiators and dispute-resolvers, too.

Recognize that emotions are involved in and guide decision-making, but strive not to let them divert you from reasoned decision processes. So acknowledge the emotions driving a disagreement. Channel your own emotions, to the extent you can, in a way that allows sufficient space and calm for making rational decisions. Even though you can't expect to control another person's high emotions, you can still help by managing your own responses and at least not fanning the flames on the other side.

2. Control: One of Stoicism's most basic charges is that we separate that which we can control from that which we cannot. Distinguishing uncontrollable externals from controlled choices just so happens to be a highly effective everyday negotiation and conflict-resolution skill, as well. If it is within your power to solve a problem or create a favorable result, then take action. However, if you are facing an obstacle over which you have no control, let it go.

3. Objectivity: Lacking an objective perspective can lead to prolonged disputes and prevent opposing sides from establishing common ground towards resolutions. When you find yourself disagreeing with someone, or in the midst of a dispute, seek objectivity. Is there an objectively right or wrong answer to the subject of your disagreement? Or is your dispute a matter of opinion, so that there's really no "right" or "wrong"?

Whenever you can find objective facts and data to shed light on a dispute, seek them out. Although it can be difficult to change a person's view of what is "true," especially with respect to closely held beliefs, it's virtually impossible to change someone's subjective opinion.

4. Humility: Humility is an under-the-radar secret weapon of some of the absolute best negotiators and problem-solvers. Humble negotiators – those who recognize that they don't necessarily know everything about a dispute and could learn from the opposing view – benefit from being open-minded and have a knack for seeing the strengths and weaknesses of their positions. Knowing what we know, as well as what we don't know, helps us define the limits of our expertise in professional and personal endeavors.

5. Empathy: Great negotiators have a knack for empathizing with their counterparts. Even when they disagree with their adversaries, and whether or not they like their opposing parties at all, these negotiators seem to be able to use empathy – an ability to walk in the shoes of others – to see conflicts from all sides.

When you empathize with someone else, and recognize the other's point of view, the person feels understood. Even more critically, the person feels *you understand*, which helps build rapport between you. And when you've built rapport and expressed empathy, you're setting yourself up to negotiate effectively and resolve conflict.

The point of all of this – and what this book explores in depth – is to focus on tools and mindsets you can use to resolve and manage conflict, negotiate, and communicate as effectively as possible, whatever the context.

Let's now take a closer look at each of the five keys, in turn. For each Stoic-inspired principle, we'll begin with a general discussion of critical concepts. Thereafter, curated writings from *The Stoic Negotiator*™ illustrate the points through narratives and actionable tips designed to help you become a better negotiator.

PRINCIPLE ONE: EMOTIONS

Sometimes, when engaged in conflict, we're going to get angry. It happens.

As a mediator, I see this regularly in professional negotiation settings. People disagree about the facts underlying a legal dispute, the reasonable settlement value of a case, or the terms of a business deal — pick your conflict — and emotions, including anger, frequently bubble up. As a result, much of my work as a negotiation facilitator involves helping individuals manage emotional responses in a way that lets them see issues more objectively and communicate effectively.

Naturally, differences of opinion with family, friends, or colleagues — or even that irritating restaurant manager, store clerk, or oblivious driver on the highway — can trigger anger. Think back to the last time you experienced that swell of frustration, or perhaps stronger feelings like ire or rage, in the heat of a disagreement or dispute. *How did you respond?*

Managing, regulating, and channeling emotion is a bedrock principle of Stoicism. In negotiation, it's very difficult to make wise decisions when we're overtaken by emotions. When tempers flare, or people get angry, upset, hurt, embarrassed . . . communication breaks down quickly and negotiations can get off track.

Processing and redirecting emotion is a principal theme

familiar to any student of Stoicism. And that theme is common among skilled negotiators and dispute-resolvers, too.

Depending on the source of the disconnect and many other variables, if involved in a heated dispute you'll likely be bombarded by emotional responses. Even if the subject matter of the underlying disagreement is of a cold, mechanical and objective nature – like a business dispute to which you have no personal attachment – it's natural that the disagreement itself will evoke an emotional response. And that's okay. You're human, after all.

But what's not okay is giving in to that emotional response and letting your brain's amygdala (the area that processes emotions) overpower your rational mind. Recognize that emotions are involved in and guide decision-making, but strive not to let them divert you from making reasoned decisions. Science suggests that though we humans are rational creatures, our primitive, "reptilian brain" sometimes leads us astray, particularly in the heat of the moment, and causes us to react in ways that can override our cooler-headed, logical brains.

In its simplest expression, the mediation formula I frequently employ is one we can also consider in day-to-day conflicts and negotiations: (1) understand, recognize, and acknowledge what a person has experienced and feels; and then (2) help focus on the person's ability to regain some control by reducing future uncertainties and forging a reasonable resolution.

Of course, we also need to realize that effective negotiation and communication requires that we both manage our own emotional responses and prepare for those we might face in a counterpart. Recognizing the emotions underlying a dispute – on both sides – is thus a vital first step.

Mediating parties who are upset or otherwise charged with emotion can find it difficult to analyze financial options clearly — like those presented in settlement negotiations — and to resist the urge to seek revenge or "get back at" the other party. Working through step "(1)," as we just discussed, can prove to be extremely demanding, though necessary, in high-emotion cases.

Noting the emotions involved in a dispute is important, but it's critical that effective negotiators then go further and identify a logical process for communicating with the other side and working toward productive resolutions to disputes. Sometimes it even takes a skilled third party, like a mediator or counselor, to intervene and help the parties manage their emotional and rational responses. However, there are certain ways we can start to manage our emotions in order to preserve our rational decision-making and negotiation skills.

If you're like most people, you've realized that it's extraordinarily difficult to make good decisions when overcome by anger. For that reason, a useful practice is training yourself to remember that the best response might very well involve some delay. Lashing out can feel right in the moment, but it's simply not conducive to problem-solving and productive conversation.

A better approach might be delaying your response, allowing anger and frustration to settle, and only then returning to discussion, bargaining, or negotiation. Easier said than done.

In these cases, do what you have to do to cool off. Take a deep breath, go for a walk, excuse yourself, or otherwise create space between you and the conflict. Write a letter or email that you never send. Pause and listen to calming music. Meditate or hit the yoga studio. You know what works best for you, and that's what matters.

Embroiled in a conflict, you will not always have the luxury of a cool-down window. But there's almost always the opportunity to gather yourself instead of reacting immediately in a way you'll later regret.

In most cases I mediate, emotions are driving the conflict on either or both sides. We all have emotional filters through which we run facts and events, and acting on emotional impulses can keep people from seeing data or a situation clearly. So in almost every situation, one of my main objectives is to help the parties move through the emotions in some manner, and then begin focusing on objective facts and potential solutions.

Being rational isn't about eliminating emotions or pretending they don't exist. It's about recognizing and channeling them to lead you towards rational clarity in decision-making.

Moreover, there's a difference between "being stoic" and "being a Stoic." While "being stoic" conjures up a stone-cold person acting without feeling, the Stoics reference something different. Stoics talk about overcoming "passions," which were viewed as more irrational, excessive to the point of unhealthy, emotions (like anger, for example). To be a Stoic is to use reason to manage our emotions and then to refocus them. An emotionless life is no good, but living controlled by passion is not much better.

We can instinctively recognize the difference between an emotionally-charged, on the one hand, and a detached and objective, on the other, attitude toward negotiation. You can imagine that when faced with making critical decisions, the cool, rational negotiator will find it easier to engage in long-term, strategic thinking — and, thus, better decision-making — than will someone operating under emotional duress.

So acknowledge the emotions driving a disagreement. Sometimes they'll be apparent, other times you might need to dig a bit through thoughtful inquiry and conversation. Channel your own emotions, to the extent you can, in a way that allows you sufficient space and calm to make rational decisions. The best negotiators manage their own emotions and, at the next level, help temper those of other decision-makers.

As a mediator, I often use a "redirection" technique to calm flared tempers. This is another tool you can try, too.

To nudge a person off a heated topic, when you sense the conversation is on the brink of becoming unproductive (or — even worse — destructive), try to redirect, or refocus, towards objectivity. One basic way to do this is to take out a pen and paper, or something like a physical or electronic whiteboard, and literally write out the points or terms underlying your disagreement. As a mediator, I might assign each party the "homework" of writing down their basic positions and interests. Sometimes it's helpful to set out, in written form, the different categories or components of an argument. Then all involved can see clearly the items upon which they agree and those remaining in dispute.

This little technique sounds very simple. It *is* very simple. And it works.

Redirecting focus from unsolvable arguments to tangible, practical action-items — things that can be more readily resolved and agreed-upon as part of a rational, fact-based conversation — both clarifies the discussion and gently moves the parties towards addressing those items they can actually control.

You can always return to the emotionally charged issues and address them as needed, and in an appropriate manner, of course. In the meantime, though, refocusing the conversation and engaging people's creative, problem-solving aptitudes can lay the groundwork for a productive solution.

Stoicism helps us develop self-control and perseverance – seeking to be unshaken, as Seneca said – that allows us to stay confident, manage emotional responses and try to steer negotiations more towards objectivity. The imagery of the undaunted negotiator, embodying the proverbial calm before the storm, is a powerful one.

Yes, you will want to react when your emotions threaten to override your better judgment. But what purpose will it serve? Even if you feel an instant of satisfaction after lashing out, what next? Does making a choice guided by anger, spite, or vengeance further your ultimate goals?

In the end, remember: We frequently can't control our circumstances. Still, even when angry or emotional, we always retain the power to control our response.

Pause, recognize, and redirect your emotions — vent, talk to a friend or a neutral party, take a break, go for a walk, or whatever — and try to guide your reaction to a calmer, rational, more objective place.

Enough to Drive You Mad

On a recent trip, I had the pleasure of renting a car. I flew thousands of miles across the country and, given that I needed transportation for a few days to explore my destination and its surroundings, reserved a rental vehicle well in advance of our travel dates.

[Caveat: I have many, many questions about the car rental industry. The list is too long even to begin to detail. For now, let's just say I'm not surprised that upstart car-sharing companies are finally disrupting what seems an incredibly inefficient and, frankly, bizarre ecosystem.]

A Little Background

I suspect it's fairly common knowledge that no rental company expects you to pay "retail" rates. That is, you need to do some form of bargain-hunting or virtual coupon-clipping before you even think about comparing prices and renting a vehicle. Whether you're privy to a group discount through membership in an organization (AAA, AARP, etc.), you've received a promotional code by email, or you're a "status" customer of a particular rental company, you have to prepare on the front end.

Why? Because — you got it — this is a negotiation opportunity. If you play your cards right, you might get a free rental day, a car class upgrade, or other special rate. And there are so many potential avenues for discounts that you simply can't even consider paying listed rates without any dispensation or perks. Otherwise, it'd be like going into a grocery or drug store, where everything is marked down as a "member price," and shopping without a free membership card. No one does that, right? (If you do, we REALLY need to talk.)

Setting The Scene

And then there's the rental counter. One thing I do know about the whole car rental process is that I always have my antennae on high alert when I approach the airport pick-up desk. This is true even if I've done all the prep work, hold a reservation and price quote in hand, and have pre-completed all requested forms.

It's always something. *Can they locate my reservation? Do they have the car I reserved? Will my car have a flat tire (yes, this has happened to me!)? Why are all of the desk associates except one taking a lunch break at 3 p.m.? How many of these existing car nicks and scratches do we need to document and photo?*

And what are all these contract provisions they want me to read and initial, considering I can't actually see them (Is there such a thing as 4-pt. font?), don't have time to read them, don't understand them, and have no realistic alternative to hurriedly signing them with my digital pen?

You Want Me To Agree To What?!?

I can sometimes access the rental agreement in advance of my appearance at the airport desk, at least to familiarize myself with the basics. When you reach the rental counter after a long flight, with dozens of people in the line behind you and everyone anxious to get the heck out of there, and you're not exactly sure what time zone you're in, it's obviously tough to dissect each line of the rental agreement. In fact, you're lucky if you can confirm even the essentials of your agreement in that environment.

Why in the world would I let you charge double the going gas price to refill my tank upon return? NO! I have my phone, so why would I need your exorbitant GPS package? NOPE! Even if I spent my entire trip crossing bridges, back and forth in an endless loop, I could never, ever, rack up enough tolls to justify your "e-toll device option," so . . . seriously?!?

Of course, as an alternative dispute resolution professional, I typically verify the presence of the arbitration clause. I do this mostly out of curiosity. You'll notice these agreement provisions are often indicated in some combination of bold, all-caps, and underlined type, perhaps paired with other preliminary dispute resolution procedure language (*e.g.*, you must take certain steps to mediate or attempt to resolve a dispute before filing an arbitration claim). The gist of it is that, if you have a dispute relating to your rental, your contract likely directs you to arbitrate in lieu of litigating before a judge and jury.

Trip Ending, Troubles Beginning

What happened at the end of my latest trip was interesting, after an otherwise uneventful driving experience over several days. As the journey concluded, I made my way through the airport parking deck maze, drove up several floors, crossed the "DANGER: DO NOT BACK UP — SEVERE TIRE DAMAGE" warnings, and pulled my vehicle into the rental return chute. A check-in employee scanned the bar code on the car's windshield and then asked me to verify the email address on his handheld digital gadget's screen.

Oddly, the address was wildly incorrect. In fact, it showed the name of a different customer, an unfamiliar rental rate, and an erroneous charge. I immediately alerted the flummoxed employee, who called his boss over to investigate. After sharing inaudible remarks and then tapping some buttons on the handheld, a few minutes later the duo announced with no explanation that they'd corrected the error.

At that point, the associate approached me again with his screen in hand, and asked me to verify the adjusted email address. That was correct, I indicated, and confirmed that he could send my receipt to this actual email address.

Whew. Glad we got that straightened out. Or so I thought.

After depositing the car, it was off to the airport. An elevator, a couple of escalators, a shuttle bus, and a walking sidewalk or two later, I made my way to the terminal. I proceeded to interact with a temperamental baggage kiosk, an even more temperamental ticketing agent, TSA security, a random search, and then several additional obstacles, before finally reaching my flight gate.

At that time, I could catch my breath. I got a bite to eat, looked at my watch, and realized I even had time to spare before boarding my flight. So I checked my email.

As promised, the car rental company had delivered my rental receipt. *Great. They actually did what they said they would.*

So What's The Catch?

Unfortunately, what I then discovered was that my car rental charge was nearly 20% higher than the amount for which I'd reserved the vehicle. *What?!?* For a week's rental, at today's rental prices, that deviation added up quickly. The tacked-on premium negated (and then some) all of the pre-rental research and price-comparing I'd done before settling on this company. I had been overcharged, and I wasn't pleased.

I had completed a great trip and had about an hour before my homebound flight departed. But this car rental thing really bothered me. I felt taken advantage of, deceived, and mistreated. I didn't want to be petty, and I certainly wasn't in the mood to ruin the last segment of my trip, but this wasn't right.

Assessing Your Options

With nearly an hour before our plane was scheduled to board, I assessed my options. Initially, I considered the easiest one: do nothing.

That's it, just move on. Is it annoying? Yes. Does it seem wrong? Yep. It's an overcharge but, in the scheme of things, is it worth spending any additional time and frustration on? Maybe it's smartest to take the "L" and let inertia do its thing.

Of course, that's not the option I chose.

The first thing I did was get my emotions in check. It would've been easy to lose my cool in that situation — and, believe me, I was teetering on the edge for a moment — but ultimately I knew that wouldn't be productive.

I was determined to keep the matter in perspective and appreciated clearly that, even in the worst case, well, it was just an overcharge. I had experienced a wonderful trip to that point and was intent not to let this little misunderstanding detract from what had otherwise been an overwhelmingly positive experience.

As far as worst alternatives to a negotiated agreement ("WATNA," in negotiation parlance) go, this one wasn't completely terrible. But what did I have to lose by trying to rectify the situation?

What's The Disconnect?

Thus, sitting at our gate, I called the rental company's customer service line. The first thing I needed to know was simple: Why was the charge greater than what we'd agreed upon? Why was I charged that additional 20%?

If you can manage your emotions and pivot towards information-gathering, logically processing the disconnect is a critical first step to resolution.

It seems such a simple point, yet in negotiation and conflict settings it can be challenging to take a step back and spotlight the source of disagreement or misunderstanding. *(1) Where do we agree, and (2) where do we see things differently?*

As to the customer service representative I got on the phone, the answers to these questions were, respectively, (1) nowhere, and (2) everywhere. I won't belabor the point, but this rep had nothing useful to share as to why the company had overcharged me. He kept making vague reference to "fees" and "taxes" and "other charges," all the while providing me no information that actually explained the discrepancy.

Are You Satisfied?

I remained calm and respectful throughout our conversation, as maddening and nonsensical as it was. At the same time, I asked the representative — directly, yet politely — to remove the overcharge. He went round and round, again talking in circles in a way that made clear he had no idea or didn't care (or perhaps neither) why the charge was incorrect.

Since apparently neither of us understands the charge, why not just remove it? That makes sense to me.

After several minutes of unproductive discussion, the rep asked to put me on hold so he could talk to his supervisor. After several more increasingly frustrating minutes, he returned and told me the best he could offer was a coupon for a 20% discount on my next car rental.

"Are you satisfied with this resolution to your issue?" the representative asked me earnestly.

"Well, no, I'm not," I replied.

I wasn't. I didn't envision using this company again after these shenanigans, so I placed little value on a hypothetical future discount. I just wanted my money back.

"This isn't right," I continued. "I appreciate what you're trying to do, but I don't understand why the charge wasn't what we'd agreed upon. I want the deal I'm supposed to have gotten up front. That's it. And I don't have a lot of time to spend on this."

As soon as I sensed I was approaching a dead end, I decided to move on. Surely this representative is a fine person, and perhaps a serviceable employee, but in this instance he was simply not solving my issue.

So I ended the conversation. Minutes later, I received a customer service email survey in my inbox.

I took a few moments to respond to the questionnaire. I answered the questions honestly, yet never rudely, and expressed displeasure with the service I'd received. Since they asked, I shared my disappointment with their company's performance. *Maybe this will help them improve their product and save other customers from experiencing what I've been dealing with here.*

If At First You Don't Succeed . . .

Meanwhile, as I calculated the remaining time before my flight's boarding, I decided I'd make one more call. Unable to let go, for some reason, I redialed the rental company's customer service number and soon was speaking with a different agent.

Once again, I calmly and coolly explained my situation and concerns regarding the overcharge.

"Wow, okay. I understand why you might be upset. Let's see what happened here so we can get this fixed. Did the previous customer service agent offer to review your itemized charges"?

Already, we were off to a 180-degree improved start. This agent immediately seemed to get it.

"I'm on my phone in the airport, so I can't really access documents very well from here. The other agent had pulled up the charges on his end, but he couldn't explain the overcharge," I relayed.

"We're going to take care of this right now," the agent stated confidently.

"Okay," she continued, while apparently reviewing my bill's details. "It looks like you were charged for an extra hour's rental.

You returned the car 31 minutes after the scheduled return."

"That timing sounds about right, I guess," I acknowledged. We had hit some traffic on the way to the airport and had been running slightly behind schedule.

"But I've been renting from this company for years, and they've always given a bit of a grace period," I continued. "And, in any case, why would they charge me for a full hour if the car was returned just 31 minutes late? Offering me a '20% off' coupon just doesn't make me feel right."

"As a matter of fact, we typically allow a 30-minute grace period. You were 31 minutes late. So what do we *do* with *you*?" the rep asked me, with a slight chuckle in her voice.

"Oh, wow. That's some luck. And I would've fallen within the acceptable period were it not for the company's own check-in glitch, which I've also explained at the beginning of this saga.

"So I think what you do is write off that extra charge and we move on with our lives. Come on, how does that sound?" I asked.

"Hmm, well, this sounds like something I can take care of in about 30 or 31 seconds. Let me reverse that extra charge. I know that's frustrating, and we don't want you to be frustrated. You'll get an email confirmation in a few minutes."

Tip-tap. Click, click. Tap, tap. I could faintly hear the familiar sound of keyboard typing over the line.

"Is there anything else I can do today to help?" concluded my new friend.

"No, thanks. You've been great, and I appreciate it," I said. And I meant it.

A few minutes later, I checked my email again. Sure enough, I had received back-to-back messages from the rental company: one with a 20% discount coupon; the other reversing the full amount of my rental overcharge.

With that, I took a deep breath, boarded my flight, and headed home.

Negotiation Takeaways

Let's recap and highlight a couple of quick takeaways here:

- **Whenever possible, keep your emotions in check and stay calm before engaging.** My philosophy is that it makes no sense to be rude or lash out at someone who can "win" simply by doing nothing. That is, in these situations, you're approaching someone you need to do something for you. So why put that person on the defensive and give him or her even less incentive to help?

- **Identify the source of your disagreement or conflict. What is it, specifically, that is causing you to see things differently?** In this case, it took me rounds of circular conversation just to figure out why my bill wasn't what I'd been expecting. Only after precisely identifying the issue (*i.e.*, the company was applying an additional 1-hour rental fee) could we begin to figure out potential solutions.

- **Persistence, persistence, persistence.** In this situation, I presented the same situation to two different reps and in an email survey response. The facts were the same in each instance, as was the customer (*i.e.*, me); the variable was the person responding to what had occurred. One person was both capable of explaining the issue and motivated to resolve it, and in the end that's all I needed.

- **You never know where your help will come from.** I've had other situations like this, as we've discussed, where a survey response triggers a prompt correction from a corporate office. It makes sense, on many levels, that the corporation would want to maintain consistent operations and keep long-time customers satisfied. But it doesn't always work that way. In my case here, I received an email reply several days after my trip, which included a kind thank-you and apology, but the corporation offered no recognition of wrongdoing or form of compensation for my troubles.

- **"May I speak with your supervisor?" actually works . . . until it doesn't.** Sometimes, you'll find that sharing feedback with a corporate office can pay direct dividends. If you're dealing with a quality company, in certain instances the corporate customer service team will go out of its way to make sure you're satisfied with your experience. In theory, they gain information that helps them improve performance, you have the opportunity to feel heard and express your concerns, and — in the best-case scenarios — you also receive fair compensation for your troubles.

- **Read your counterpart, and get in synch when possible.** In my conversation with the second agent, at one point she gave a slight chuckle. Along with that hint, she spoke in just enough of a tongue-in-cheek manner that I gambled and injected a bit of humor into our banter. Whereas the first rep with whom I spoke was a dud, the second was a breath of fresh air. Our instant rapport was just enough to lighten the mood, let us see each other as actual human beings, and finally help resolve a relatively silly misunderstanding in a productive way.

It Doesn't Have to Upset You

*"You don't have to turn this into something.
It doesn't have to upset you."*
—Marcus Aurelius

You're convinced you're right, but for some reason the other side just doesn't get it. You've explained your position over and over again, but you're still not making progress.

You know the feeling. The mobile phone provider insists on charging you that international fee for a service you switched off three months ago, again a month ago, and a third time last week. Your ten-year-old still doesn't get why playing video games for 8 hours on a beautiful spring Saturday is a bad thing. The attorney on the other side of your mediation is looking at the same medical report you are, but for some reason what to you looks like a slam-dunk at trial to her is a reason to investigate your client for fraud.

Either they aren't listening, they don't understand what you're saying, or maybe they don't even care about your point of view. Meanwhile, the clock is ticking, you feel like you're wasting time talking to your counterpart, and pressure to reach a constructive resolution seems to be intensifying by the minute.

It's incredibly frustrating, right? If you're like most people, these scenarios probably make you, at minimum, anxious, frustrated, or both.

Depending on the source of the disconnect and many other variables, if involved in such a situation while mediating or negotiating you'll likely be bombarded by emotional responses. Even if the subject matter of the underlying disagreement is of a cold, mechanical and objective nature – like a business matter to which you have no personal attachment – it's natural that the disagreement itself will evoke an emotional response. And that's okay. You're human, after all.

But what's not okay is giving in to that emotional response and letting your amygdala overpower your brain's rational response. Recognize that emotions are involved in and guide decision-making, but don't let them divert you from making reasoned decisions.

Science teaches us that though we humans are rational creatures, our primitive, "reptilian brain" sometimes leads us astray, particularly in the heat of the moment, and causes us to react in ways that can override our cool-headed, logical brains. Although our amygdala-centered, emotion-based limbic system has helped maintain the survival of the human species for millions of years – no small feat! – it's not going to keep you calm and collected during a heated negotiation.

I've rarely, if ever, seen a hot, emotional exchange between disputing parties lead directly to rational discourse and decision-making during a negotiation. It doesn't work with your kids or your spouse, it doesn't score you any "wins" when commenting on provocative social media posts, and it certainly doesn't result in compromise from your negotiating counterpart.

Again, recognizing the emotions involved is important, but it's critical that effective negotiators then go further and identify a logical process for communicating with the other side and working toward productive resolutions to disputes. There are various ways we can do this, and frequently it takes a skilled third party, like a mediator, to intervene and help the parties manage their emotional and rational responses.

So acknowledge the emotions at play – both in your counterpart and in you – and then process them and take rational action to further resolution between the parties. When your emotions overtake you, in personal or professional disputes, your chances of reaching a satisfactory agreement on any matter plummet. This approach is very difficult to master, and you alone might not be able to control your emotions all the time, but these skills can be improved with practice and hard work.

Want to Make Your Life Easier?

As a mediator, I'm always prepared to encounter stoked emotions when I step in to help resolve a dispute. Emotions, disagreements, conflict, frustration, anger . . . some or all of these are bound to emerge, in varying degrees, in the context of a lawsuit.

Part of my job is to help defuse these reactions and guide the parties from opposing viewpoints towards more productive conversation. So I fully expect friction and discord whenever I begin to unpack a case.

This is normal and completely fine — we're humans, after all — and sometimes parties simply need to vent. They come to mediation, talk to a neutral party, and feeling "heard" alone can begin to heal the wounds of an aggrieved party. Skilled attorneys help their clients by examining a case through the lens of relevant facts and applicable law — that is, the more objective and verifiable elements of the dispute — so that the parties can move from focusing on past transgressions to joint problem-solving and forward-looking analyses.

On a personal level, some (all?) of us have had distressing disagreements and arguments with family or friends during which, in the heat of the moment, someone finally stops and says, "Hey, what are we arguing about, anyway?" Maybe you've gotten fired up during an unpleasant conversation with a customer service representative who can't seem to understand why you want to get what you actually paid for three weeks ago (go figure!). Or perhaps your teenager argues with virtually anything you say and drives you and your spouse bonkers.

Blurting out insults rarely makes a dispute better and, if

anything, will make it worse. We all know this, yet sometimes we just can't help but dig ourselves deeper into a hole. Soon enough, you're exchanging barbs, the cycle of emotional reactions accelerates, and your conversation goes hopelessly off the rails.

Look, it's going to happen sometimes. The point I try to make with reactive litigants, applicable also in non-legal contexts, is one that harkens back to the Stoics: Yes, you will want to react when your emotions threaten to override your better judgment. But what purpose will it serve? Even if you feel better for an instant after lashing out, what next? Does making a choice guided by anger, spite, or vengeance further your ultimate goals?

We always have the choice of how to respond. Pause, recognize, and redirect your emotions — vent, talk to a friend or a neutral party, take a break, go for a walk, or whatever — and try to guide your reaction to a calmer, rational, more objective place.

This practice will serve as a key step to helping you manage conflict more productively. With it, your life might very well become easier — certainly worth a try — and it most definitely will be more pleasant.

Don't Be That Person

"Always shun that which makes you angry."
— Publilius Syrus

"I'll tell you one thing. I'm never mediating with *that guy (or woman)* again. Not after *this* negotiation!"

I've heard this, and X-rated versions of the sentiment, uttered after a mediation more times than I'd like to admit. When I observe one attorney say this about his or her counterpart, I feel sorry for the lawyers and, even more so, for their clients. Of course, all along the way, I do whatever I can to keep things calm and civil, and even to preserve or rehabilitate the offending party's reputation.

Sometimes, though, you can't save people from themselves. In a negotiation, if a person places little value on the parties' ongoing relationship, their own reputation, or both, then that negotiator is apt to sacrifice everything to attempt a short-term gain. When it goes well, those gamblers might extract immediate value at the expense of their long-term success; when it goes poorly, well, they run the risk of losing both a potential deal *and* their good graces.

Just the other day, at the close of a mediation, I witnessed a scenario like the latter. Two volatile attorneys, who entered negotiations as bitter rivals, unfortunately left as sworn enemies. Things went from bad to worse, with the sides ultimately concluding that they'd never trust each other to negotiate ever again.

Fortunately, mediations like this are rare. However, you've all probably had a negotiation or difficult interaction with someone, in your professional or personal spheres, with whom you'd prefer to deal never again.

Negotiation: Sources Of Disconnect

When disagreements intensify at my mediations, I can typically dissect the problem with reference to one or more of these basic areas of dissatisfaction stemming from the interaction: substantive, procedural, and emotional/psychological.

- *Substantive differences* can occur when attorneys or their clients on either side view a case value or its legal underpinnings differently. In this category of disagreement, most professionals can have reasonable differences of opinion without taking things personally or getting terribly upset. Conflict can be healthy, and perhaps some matters simply must be decided by a judge or jury. Of course, there are times when parties become so entrenched in their beliefs that they refuse to accept even the possibility that they could be wrong, or that a judge or jury could see things differently. I like to stress to parties the importance of humility in negotiations because, after all, it's not easy to predict the future. Most experienced attorneys understand this, and they use that understanding to assess risk and make sound negotiating decisions on behalf of their clients.

- *Procedural problems* arise when parties or their lawyers have differing ideas about the negotiation process and how bargaining is to occur. Some people negotiate well together, others less so. You can call this negotiation "chemistry," or lack thereof, that some relationships share and others simply miss. One party might be less forthcoming than the other, and yet another could be more prone to arguing over minutiae than to collaborating in search of compromise. Various differences in negotiation style and preference can lead to procedural conflict in a mediation setting and, though these differences cause tension and struggle during negotiations, an experienced mediator can often help smooth the process and overcome procedural disconnects. In business contexts and in everyday negotiations, too, you can use empathy cues to help relate to your counterpart's style and approach and, ideally, to communicate in a way that allows your counterpart to process your messages clearly.

- A third category of problem tends to result in the most damaging, explosive types of conflict at mediation. **Emotional and psychological incompatibility** can lead to displays of frustration, anger, extreme impatience, irritability, and hostility that will derail even the most promising negotiations. These are the negotiations that can harm relationships and cause parties to fight, rather than compromise, over issues they could otherwise agree to substantively, leading to unnecessary wastes of time and money. Furthermore, the combatant parties can wind up inflicting and sustaining emotional harm that benefits no one and lessens the chances of resolution in the underlying case — and potentially in future cases in which the attorneys or the parties will be involved.

Consider these three broad categories of conflict. Which you do encounter in your negotiations or conflicts, and how to you handle them?

Undoubtedly, we all want to avoid being *that person*. Let's face it: you might have great points to make, but you won't get very far if no one wants to deal with you!

Substantive differences and procedural matters can frequently be overcome, or at least managed, with a bit of work. People operating rationally can have different views on relevant facts and circumstances, and sometimes the best you can do is "agree to disagree." Procedural and stylistic disconnects, too, can often be massaged to facilitate discourse even in the face of different approaches and negotiation tendencies.

Controlling Emotions And Mitigating Damage

The emotional blowups and, frankly, nasty exchanges that sometimes result in the heat of an argument can, unfortunately, result in both short- and long-term damage if they get out of hand. The last thing you want to do is sabotage your conflict resolution efforts — in your present and potentially future engagements — because you alienate your counterpart or otherwise harm your relationship to the point of effectively cutting lines of communication.

So let's state the obvious: To avoid being the person no one wants to engage in dispute resolution efforts, it's helpful to avoid unhealthy conflict with others at the negotiation table. The good news is that these most harmful areas of discord can often be avoided. Still, it's not easy to manage emotions, keep your cool under fire, and maintain a clear, rational head in an adversarial setting. This is true even in the collaborative framework mediation provides, more conducive to cooperation than what you'd confront in the courtroom.

No One Wants To Be "That Person"

Yes, there are ways you can work on controlling emotions and engaging your rational, problem-solving tools. We've talked about some of those basic tools before, like delay, deep listening and asking questions, aiming to be unshaken, and separating personal and business decisions, to name just a few.

The point is that though certain circumstances and realities of a dispute are out of our control, we always retain a choice about how to respond. At best, we can employ responses that smooth over heated moments or flared tempers; at worst, we can respond in a way that at least doesn't provoke further discord.

And it's easy to dismiss this stuff as "touchy-feely" or not worth your effort. But before doing that, consider that I've seen literally millions of settlement dollars squandered, over my years as a mediator, as a direct result of attorneys' failure to use their rational judgment upon being overpowered by their emotional reactions to the personalities on the other side of the table. Remember, too, that these are professionals paid precisely to negotiate! The tragedy in so many of those cases is that just a fraction of the parties' disagreements were about matters of substance; rather, their inflammatory exchanges were the determining impediment.

You probably come across instances like these in your own professional and personal lives, too. *What are we even arguing about?* How often is the cause of conflict in the communication, or the reaction, rather than the underlying subject of a disagreement?

So don't be that person. It's okay if you can't always agree on substance, and procedural preferences can often be accommodated or at least tweaked to the point of compatibility between professionals.

But be smart, and let cool heads prevail. Concluding a negotiation with the other side swearing to never again mediate or engage with you is an instant loss for you (and your client) and unquantifiable future losses to you (and your future clients). Erupting during a heated discussion with friends or family that leaves hurt feelings, bitterness, or worse . . . is losing your cool worth it?

There's always *that person* we have to deal with. But must it be you?

Anger's Best Remedy

"Delay is the greatest remedy for anger."
—Seneca

I recently noticed this excerpt from our local youth soccer club's posted "parent policy":

DO NOT contact your coach or director until 24 hours after a game/training ends if there is an issue to discuss. Approaching the coach while frustrated never helps. Please be courteous and respectful.

Putting aside concerns about why such a directive is needed in the first place — this is kids playing soccer! — let's focus on the policy's broader principle. The message is consistent with Seneca's observation that we can quell anger by allowing the passage of time.

And this point is one we can use to help manage daily conflict of all sorts. Because here's the problem: *When anger overtakes you, making logical, sound decisions is virtually impossible.*

Engaged in conflict, we're going to get angry sometimes. It happens. As a mediator, I see this regularly in professional negotiation settings. People disagree about the facts underlying a legal dispute, the reasonable settlement value of a case, or the terms of a business deal — pick your conflict — and emotions, including anger, frequently bubble up. As a result, much of my work as a negotiation facilitator involves helping individuals manage emotional responses in a way that lets them see issues more objectively and communicate effectively.

Naturally, differences of opinion with family, friends, or colleagues — or even that irritating restaurant manager, store clerk, or oblivious driver on the highway — can trigger anger. Think back to the last time you experienced that swell of frustration, or perhaps stronger feelings like ire or rage, in the heat of a disagreement or dispute. How did you respond?

If you're like most people, you've realized that it's extraordinarily difficult to make good decisions when overcome by anger. The threshold challenge is remembering that *the best response might very well be delay*. Lashing out can feel right in the moment, but it's simply not conducive to problem-solving and productive conversation.

A better approach will often be delaying your response, allowing anger and frustration to settle, and only then returning to discussion, bargaining, or negotiation. Easier said than done.

So do what you have to do. Take a deep breath, go for a walk, excuse yourself, or otherwise create space between you and the conflict. Write a letter or email that you never send. Pause and listen to calming music. Meditate, pump some iron, or hit the yoga studio. You know what works best for you, and that's what matters.

Embroiled in a conflict, you will not always have the luxury of a 24-hour cool-down window, like the parents seething to curse out the youth soccer coaches. But there's almost always the opportunity to gather yourself instead of reacting immediately in a way you'll later regret.

And, finally: We frequently can't control our circumstances. Still, even when angry, *we always retain the power to control our response*.

Separating the People from the Problem . . . and from Each Other

"However he may treat me, I must deal rightly by him. This is what lies with me, what none can hinder."
— Epictetus

"Separating the people from the problem" is a key that Roger Fisher and William Ury, and many of their disciples in the mediation and negotiation field, discuss as a fundamental *Getting to Yes* principle.[2]

And with good reason: Focusing on the objective issues in dispute, rather than bogging down in personal attacks and emotion-driven arguments, tends to be imminently more effective in negotiation settings.

Identifying Your Pressure Points

At the negotiating table, separating the people from the problem is critical. And as I was reminded when mediating a recent lawsuit involving high emotions, sometimes it is also imperative to separate – quite literally – the people *from each other* as part of this approach.

You'll recall that mediation is a structured negotiation process, whereby a neutral party – the mediator – helps parties to a dispute negotiate towards a mutually agreeable resolution. The mediator, unlike a judge or arbitrator, does not make a decision or tell the parties what to do; rather, the mediator guides opposing sides to uncover their best settlement options.

In this instance, the parties called upon me to mediate an injury case.

As each litigant explained to me its perspective in separate, private pre-mediation calls, it became apparent that the plaintiff/employee and the defendant/insurance company really had no bad blood between them. The employee had been injured on the job, and the employer's insurer wanted to resolve her case in a reasonable settlement package.

But it was more complicated than that.

Unfortunately, the case had become emotionally charged because of rocky past interactions, as I came to learn, between people on the peripheries of the dispute. The employee's daughter, understandably concerned about her mother's well-being, had been heavily involved in day-to-day management of the case. And she ruffled many feathers within the operations of both the employer and its insurer. In fact, the insurance company adjuster in charge of the claim – the person controlling the money – absolutely *hated* the daughter. She believed the daughter was rude, causing friction between the employee and her company, and just plain unreasonable.

Furthermore, I learned that one of the insurance company's attorneys was a young, ambitious lawyer who clearly wanted to make a name for himself within his new law firm. But his litigation tactics leading up to the mediation were not appreciated by opposing counsel. The plaintiff's lawyer told me, point blank, that this eager defense attorney had been acting like such a *&%^ that he had given up all direct communication with the guy. Though another seemingly peripheral problem, a difficult lawyer on either side can completely gum up an otherwise promising negotiation.

Crafting A Work-Around

Luckily, once tricky elements like these become clear, we

can often work around them when we effectively diagnose and then dissect a problem at mediation. First, after the plaintiff's attorney had confided in me that the mediation would work more smoothly if the employee's daughter was not directly involved in the negotiations, the attorney and his client – with my support – successfully (and artfully) suggested to the daughter that she wait in the lobby during the mediation and keep her distance from the opposing side.

Additionally, when we spoke prior to the mediation session, the defense partner agreed that he would join his eager associate at the mediation. That way, we figured, the young attorney most familiar with the case would be part of the process, but the senior lawyer – whom I knew to be knowledgeable, reasonable and level-headed – would oversee the mediation and ensure that the negotiations were run appropriately and without unneeded puffery or bravado.

Again: Separate The People From The Problem.

With the daughter and the junior attorney insulated from creating further conflict, the parties were able to focus on the substantive dispute and resolved it through the mediation process. We discovered that the parties' underlying disagreements were actually quite few, and the majority of the pre-mediation friction, indeed, quickly dissipated once we separated the daughter and the attorney who had been generating it.

Observations And Takeaways

This mediation anecdote highlights a couple of key points to keep in mind during any negotiation:

- Separating the people from the problem is an effective

strategy that helps negotiators focus on substance and remain objective. In many instances, a dispute is more about the personalities involved than the underlying facts or disagreement.

- Conflict can be challenging, yes. There will be times when you and a counterpart see things so differently that you think a resolution is forever out of reach. However, you'll never know if you can agree on the underlying substance if you're stuck on extraneous personal or procedural matters. At minimum, your job as a negotiator should include channeling your emotions in a manner effective enough to allow you to explore points of genuine agreement and disagreement.

- As a general rule, it's important to involve relevant decision-makers in the negotiation process. At the same time, when you can identify individuals or groups likely to distract from productive conversation – by igniting bad feelings, arousing negative emotions, or tending to argue more than collaborate, for instance – determine ways to minimize their adversarial postures and negativity.

- Using a neutral party or, in some instances, even a tactical ally on the opposing side, you might find creative ways to defuse anticipated clashes. In some cases, this could include physically keeping emotional parties in separate locations, communicating by phone or video instead of negotiating face-to-face (*i.e.*, in the same "in real life" locale), or removing destructive, non-essential personalities from the conversation.

You might view conflict resolution as peeling the layers of

an onion, or perhaps as putting together the pieces of a puzzle. Ultimately, when you identify incompatible personalities or people whose toxic mix threatens to poison a negotiation, separating those people, where possible, will help you focus on the actual dispute and work more efficiently toward resolution.

Personal Feelings, Business Decisions

> *"You shouldn't give circumstances the power to rouse anger, for they don't care at all."*
> —Marcus Aurelius

It's their fault I'm injured, and I'm going to make them pay. I'll drag this lawsuit out as long as it takes, and I don't care how much it costs me. Maybe I win, maybe I lose. But I promise I'll push this all the way to the Supreme Court. They're messing with the wrong guy.

Recognizing The Personal And The Emotional

I sometimes hear sentiments like this when I mediate cases involving injured parties. Expressions of anger, frustration, sadness, rage, embarrassment, and fear aren't always this extreme or obvious. But you can find the feelings if you know where to look.

For an injured party in settlement negotiations with a belligerent defendant or insurance company, these responses are natural and to be expected.

You know what I mean. Suppose someone has suffered a legitimate injury that causes physical pain and an inability to work and earn a full wage. Suppose further that the person is angry — furious, even — at her former employer, and its insurance company, because she's lost her job, she still hurts, her lack of income means she's under pressure to pay her overdue mortgage and avoid foreclosure, and she doesn't like the assigned insurance company doctor. And on top of all that (and perhaps much more), she has to deal with a confusing legal system, an uncertain future, a cranky insurance adjuster, and a bunch of lawyers.

When faced with cases like these, as a mediator I try to enable people to manage their emotions and preserve their ability to negotiate wisely. Since we can't undo the past, as much as we might like to, how can we regain a sense of control, most effectively pick up the pieces and move ahead?

Acknowledgement And Refocus

In its simplest form, the mediation formula I frequently employ is one we can also consider in day-to-day conflicts: (1) understand, recognize, and acknowledge what a person has experienced and feels; and then (2) help focus on the person's ability to regain some control by reducing future uncertainties and forging a reasonable resolution.

Mediating parties who are upset or otherwise charged with emotion can find it difficult to analyze financial options clearly — like those presented in settlement negotiations — and to resist the urge to seek revenge or "get back at" the other party. When that happens, people say things like the quote at the top of this piece, seemingly prepared to forego potentially beneficial settlement possibilities in order to exact some measure of payback. Working through the aforementioned step "(1)" can prove to be extremely demanding, though necessary, in high-emotion cases.

By contrast, an insurance adjuster, for instance, is much less likely to have an overriding emotional component involved in a settlement decision. That is, for the insurance company, it's predominantly a business decision: a matter of dollars, cents, and closing a file. Unless it has been particularly memorable, the case at hand is just one of hundreds or thousands an adjuster must manage at a given time.

To the insurance adjuster or business executive, the injured party may be simply a name on a file and a claim number. The calculation consists of crunching numbers, statistical analysis, evaluating budgets, and quantifying monetary fund reserves. For the company, the negotiation exercise is virtually always more straightforward by comparison, because it's "nothing personal, all business."

Towards Objectivity And A Business-Like Approach

We can instinctively recognize the difference between an emotionally-charged, on the one hand, and a detached and objective, on the other, attitude toward negotiation. The respective approaches taken by the injured individual and the adjuster illustrate this well.

You can imagine that when faced with making critical decisions, the cool, rational negotiator will find it easier to engage in long-term, strategic thinking — and, thus, better decision-making — than will someone operating under emotional duress.

The contrast here gives us something to draw upon in our daily conflicts, as well. The next time you're engaged in a dispute, consider: Can you compartmentalize your personal feelings and your "business decisions"? Recognizing what you can control and what you cannot, can you empathize with and acknowledge the other side, and then move to explore rational resolution options? On an even deeper level, can you recognize *your own* emotions that might impact your decision-making process, and then manage *them* in a constructive way to minimize conflict?

These are challenging tasks in our daily lives, to be sure, just like it might be challenging for an injured party mediating to resolve an emotional lawsuit.

For those seeking to overcome the challenge, and negotiate more like a Stoic might: *Can you separate the emotional and the objective — the "personal" and the "business" — and improve your decision-making habits?*

Negotiation and the Art of Impulse Control

"It is essential that we not respond impulsively . . . take a moment before reacting and you will find it is easier to maintain control."
— *Epictetus*

Managing emotions in negotiation and conflict settings is a recurring topic here at *The Stoic Negotiator*. And with good reason: When anger overtakes you, making logical, sound decisions is virtually impossible.

Managing The Emotional Response

Filtering emotional responses in the face of conflict helps us see issues more objectively and communicate effectively. Stoic principles are a useful guide as we face this challenge, because Stoicism teaches recognizing and redirecting our emotions to avoid destructive actions precipitated by anger. These logical principles of emotion regulation present goals worth emulating.

Seven Tips You Can Use

As a practical matter, though, this question frequently arises: *In the heat of a dispute, how can we recognize and compartmentalize our emotions before acting upon them?*

In other words: *How do I keep from losing my cool and destroy our chances of reaching a resolution?*

You probably have approaches you tend to rely on when the going gets tough in a negotiation or conflict setting. If you're looking for other ideas that might help:

1. **Prepare.** Every effective negotiation begins with preparation. Of course, ideally, you should research the substance of your discussion and know it backwards and forwards. (*What's the market price for cars of this type? What real estate comps are available for houses like yours? What's a realistic salary range for the job you're seeking?*) For bonus points, you should know your counterpart's position as well as or better than he or she does, too. But you can also poise yourself to counter more subjective facets of an anticipated interaction, including your own emotional responses. These words from Marcus Aurelius are helpful, particularly when you're about to engage with a difficult person or situation: "When you wake up in the morning, tell yourself: The people I deal with today will be meddling, ungrateful, arrogant, dishonest, jealous, and surly." There are plenty of wonderful people out there. Still, we can't be so naive as to think that all is rainbows and unicorns in the negotiation world. We can, however, be ready for the conflict, choose to take the high road, lead with empathy, and resist the temptation to respond in kind.

Marcus Aurelius also taught: "To live a good life: We have the potential for it. If we learn to be indifferent to what makes no difference." Perhaps the Stoic precursor to the ubiquitous "don't sweat the small stuff" advice headlining millions of motivational break room posters and memes, this idea has been around at least thousands of years. The enduring point is that we retain the option not to get riled up about things that don't matter. It takes circumspection and tremendous awareness to know what makes a difference and what makes none, of course, and that leads us back to the value of preparation.

2. **Count it out.** Before responding to an inflammatory remark or situation, recite the alphabet to yourself, as Stoic Athenodorus Cananites famously advised the emperor Octavian; if you prefer numbers, count to ten. As Thomas Jefferson said, "When angry, count 10 before you speak; if very angry, 100." Think of this as placing yourself in a time-out, if you'd like. During the pause it takes to go through the letters or numbers, you give yourself a chance to cool off and delay a knee-jerk response you might later regret.

3. **Breathe.** Take deep breaths, perhaps even incorporating deliberate breathing into your counting or alphabet recitation. Though you might be tempted to write this off as too obvious to be effective, give it a try. I'll admit I was at first skeptical myself, but after reading enough studies and hearing so many advocates for controlled breathing techniques, I opened my mind and became a believer.

4. **Be silent.** You often don't *have* to respond immediately to a negotiation proposal or verbal barb, so take your time and gather your thoughts. Give yourself space to process what's been done or said and formulate

how you'd like to proceed. Silence can feel awkward, but with patience you can use it to your strategic advantage. Meanwhile, the other party will be tempted to fill the conversation gap and perhaps either give you more valuable information or, at least, vent off any remaining steam. Either way, a dose of silence may ultimately move you towards more productive communication.

5. **Call for a break.** If you need and are able to, physically remove yourself from the conflict or heated negotiation. Propose to the other person that perhaps a break would be helpful. If you'd like, excuse yourself for a few minutes (or days, or weeks, depending on the circumstances), or suggest that taking a pause might allow everyone to regroup and return with a fresh perspective. *Take a walk.* Specifics of each situation, of course, will help dictate the appropriate transition to an opportunity to stretch your legs and maybe get some fresh air. *Grab a cup of coffee or tea.* Walking down the hall or around the block is a great way to reset your conversation, and even light physical activity like taking a stroll can do wonders for your negotiating and problem-solving stamina. *Meditate or listen to music while you walk*, if that's your thing. *Relax your shoulders, roll your neck, stretch your fingers . . .* again, whatever works best for you. A well-timed break can give you a new perspective when you return to focus on resolving your dispute.

6. **Quiz yourself.** Before you respond to someone or something that has you on the verge of anger, ask yourself: *Will this matter in ten minutes? Ten hours? How about ten days, or even ten years?* So that driver cut you off in traffic. In the moment, it can feel like a direct attack, threat, or challenge. Your competitive

juices flow and adrenaline courses through your veins. Tempting as it might be, you don't *need* to respond in a way that escalates a potential conflict. Then even ten *seconds* later, you might be ready to move on and never see that oblivious motorist again in your life. As you know, were you unable to manage your response, a split-second angry reaction could be extremely costly. Likewise, if someone offends you with a lowball initial offer at the negotiating table, a quick reaction could blow up your potential to consummate a profitable deal. On the other hand, if you're able to move past your initial urge to punch back and instead focus on the big picture, your self-discipline could be the difference between sure failure and long-term success.

7. **Take perspective.** Before you react, consider what your kids/parents/partner would think if they were watching. What kind of example do you want to set for them, or how would they expect you to act? And what type of person do you want to be?

Another way to get there: How would your inner child, the 10-year-old you, want you *now* to respond in this moment? What about the 100-year-old you, looking back in time? What advice might those past and future versions of yourself offer?

These are deep, powerful questions, and conflict gives us daily opportunities to turn our aspirations into actions. As wise Epictetus said, "Don't explain your philosophy. Embody it."

Guiding your emotions to maximize your decision-making abilities can be a lifelong practice. These are just a few tools you might find helpful along the way, particularly in negotiating or resolving conflict.

PRINCIPLE TWO: CONTROL

One of Stoicism's most basic charges is that we separate that which we can control from that which we cannot. Distinguishing uncontrollable externals from controlled choices just so happens to be a highly effective everyday negotiation and conflict-resolution skill, as well.

Control: If it is within your power to solve a problem or create a favorable result, then take action. However, if you are facing an obstacle over which you have no control, let it go.

A central teaching theme of Epictetus, the renowned Stoic, is distinguishing what is in our control from what is not in our control. This a tremendously powerful concept, and to anyone familiar with the Serenity Prayer this will sound familiar.

Can I Change It, Or Not?

In fact, this directive sets forth an essential — if not *the most essential* — philosophical tenet of Stoicism. Separating those things we can control from what we cannot. Identifying what is worth trying to change, and what is futile. Focusing our efforts and attention on what we can do, in each present moment, to move closer to our goals.

Of course, so many aspects of life are truly out of our control, and what remains is to react and manage our options as best we can. This is true for us in negotiation, too.

Sometimes, you're in conflict with someone who might be persuaded to see things your way. Or perhaps you're trying to unravel a problem with many facets that requires you to collaborate with another person, or perform extra work, or maybe do something else that can push you towards your goal.

Return to the "control" question throughout the negotiation process. Distinguishing uncontrollable externals from controlled choices just so happens to be a highly effective everyday negotiation and conflict-resolution skill, as well. If it is within your power to solve a problem or create a favorable result, then take action. However, if you are facing an obstacle over which you have no control, then let it go.

Certainly, it requires practice to train yourself to ask, in the face of a challenging dispute with a difficult adversary, these critical questions: Is this something (or, someone) I can control? And, if not, how can I control my choices with respect to this immovable force and reach the best possible outcome?

If you can impact a result, then choose your approach. When you determine your obstacle is truly unmovable, and you have no power to control the result, reassess your options. True wisdom lies in knowing the difference between the controllable and the inevitable.

In negotiation, it's always important to know what's possible and negotiable — for you and for your counterpart — and what's simply unchangeable. That is, you must identify what you can control.

Additionally, good negotiators know that they're most effective when able to think clearly and free of provocation. When you feel yourself tempted to bark back at an angry counterpart, no matter what that person says or does, you have the power to choose a different response.

It's never easy to resist or respond calmly in the face

of someone or something that generates a strong emotional reaction, as we've discussed previously. Unfortunately, we rarely make our best decisions under duress or reacting in haste. Exercising patience, judgement, and restraint is often not the path of least resistance.

It's a natural tendency to react under negotiation pressure and either give in to frustration or respond reflexively. Nonetheless, that response is yours to make, and you alone control which path you choose.

These notions of what we can and can't control apply to *how we approach the individuals with whom we are in conflict or in negotiations*, too. In our daily lives, we encounter people who we might think are flawed. Maybe you have a selfish uncle, or a rude landlord, or a former spouse or partner in your life that gives you grief. We interact with strangers all of the time, too, and — let's face it — those encounters aren't all pleasant.

But what's the point of dwelling on others' imperfections? Does it bring you closer to your goal?

In mediations, I try to help people see that focusing on others' faults (as they perceive them) is counter-productive. You can use this concept when you're negotiating or trying to persuade, too. Instead of wishing that the company rep was a better person, that your ex- wasn't so selfish, or that your opposition wasn't behaving so irrationally, refocus on how you react and respond.

Finally, remember that one thing we can never, ever control is the passage of time. You know this, but here let's focus on its connection specifically to negotiation. Frequently, I notice negotiating parties becoming sidetracked by dwelling on past events that they'd love to undo. *If only I hadn't*, or *if they just would've done it right last year* . . . . But, of course, just like we know it's pointless to cry over spilt milk, there's no way to reverse the past.

That's why negotiation is most effective when it's forward-focused. When you're engaged and negotiating with someone, you clearly can't control the events that brought you to that moment. They're gone, so acknowledge them, process them, and let them go. Instead, focus on moving forward from where you are, resolving the challenges before you, and look to the future.

I find in a lot of disputes that one party or another gets hung up on things that are frustrating but either irrelevant or uncontrollable.

- *Why is this person being so difficult?*
- *Why couldn't they have handled this correctly from the beginning?*
- *Why did that THING have to happen in the first place?*
- *Looking to the future, do you really KNOW what's going to happen at trial?*

Sometimes people get fixated on past events, and it eats at them to the point that they're unable to make good decisions going forward. Prior occurrences are the quintessential "uncontrollables." You know, those words we can't un-say, the bells we can't un-ring, and that toothpaste we can't stuff back into the tube.

That's why negotiation, along with conflict and dispute resolution, are at the core forward-looking. To the extent we use negotiation and collaboration to take control of what we can, with an eye towards the future, we must also resist becoming stuck in the past.

For those negotiating to resolve lawsuits, control means accepting the person on the other side of the table, accepting what's happened (*e.g.*, an injury, dispute) and then figuring out how best to persevere and move forward.

That's a basic formula we can apply in everyday conflicts, too.

Who's in Control Here?

> *"The chief task in life is simply this: to identify and separate matters so that I can say clearly to myself which are externals not under my control, and which have to do with the choices I actually control. Where then do I look for good and evil? Not to uncontrollable externals, but within myself to the choices that are my own."*
> — Epictetus

Recall a foundational principle of Stoicism that lies at the core of the philosophy's teachings:

Separate what you can control from what you cannot, and focus on the former.

The "dichotomy of control" leaves negotiators a critical framework to help guide our decision-making.

Bargaining For Control

How do we employ this powerful lens in everyday negotiation settings? Let's explore a couple of strategic and tactical points that draw on the vital control concept Epictetus laid out.

We'd noted previously that in negotiations, often people become fixated on things that happened in the past, and who did what to whom, and it eats at them to the point that they're unable to make good decisions going forward.

Of course, we can't control the past, what other people think of us, or their conflict styles, or even our gut emotional reactions that come up in difficult situations. But no matter what happens, we are always in control of our response.

Now let's take this idea a bit further. Yes, the control dichotomy gives us an opportunity to concentrate our energies and efforts most productively. You've also probably observed that people generally prefer to be in control of their negotiation outcomes than to rely on luck or someone else's decision-making.

One of the reasons litigants prefer mediation — structured negotiation processes — over going to court is that they'd rather control their outcomes, to the extent possible, than rely on an unknown and unpredictable judicial process. Have you considered why the entire insurance industry exists? To help people control risks. You pay relatively smaller amounts up front, or over time, to avoid potentially greater losses in the future. On the flip side, would you prefer to receive $95 today or $100 a year from now? You'd probably rather control the money sooner rather than later, and you might even pay for that privilege.

Control: Using The Force!

For our purposes here, let's assume that the preference for control is an underlying (or overt) force in most people's desired negotiation outcomes. Now, since we know people like to feel in control, you can incorporate this into your negotiation strategies and tactics.

Here's a tip: Give choices when you can, and let the other side or entity choose from acceptable options. This allows your counterpart a sense of control, which itself can create opportunities for both sides to "win" a negotiation.

A few points to illustrate:

- *"We can pay $90K today, or $100K over time. Which would you prefer?"*

- *"Should we pay $10K to you directly, or would you rather we use our leverage with the creditor and pay $5K to settle your outstanding bill?"*

- *Wherever you land, let the other side feel like the solution was theirs. Sometimes you can get there by asking the right set of open-ended questions.*

Assuming you are relatively indifferent as to which option the other side chooses, offers like these perform double-duty. Importantly, they confer value that's both tangible (*i.e.*, the money or thing you'd provide or perform) and intangible (*i.e.*, that valuable sense of control).

The notion of choice and control is interesting and will certainly be familiar to parents. Who hasn't posed some version of this question to your toddler: "What would you like to eat first, your broccoli or your peas?" In this classic example of giving an option, either way the parent gets a win. The key is that the child gains a feeling of control in the outcome and that, often, is enough to nudge towards a desirable result (as opposed to trying to force the child to eat vegetables against his or her will).

In everyday negotiation scenarios, for grown-ups, too, exercising choice gives us a feeling of power and control. And, yes — let's be honest — we tend to like that.

Is It Magic? Well . . . Not Exactly!

Another way to think about this: Have you heard of a technique called equivocation? I read about this recently and couldn't help but think of negotiation and control principles.

Equivocation (or, "magician's choice") is a device any sorcerer worth his or her salt regularly calls upon to steer unsuspecting audience participants and execute tricks with apparent ease.

The gist: A magic performer deals two cards on a table and asks a volunteer to select one. Suppose the trick depends on the subject choosing the card on the left. If the person points to the card on the left, our wizard will hand the card to the volunteer. *Okay, great. The card in your hand is yours.* If subject indicates the card on the right, the performer will take that card up and leave the other card to be the volunteer's.

Result: *In either case, the volunteer receives the intended card!*

What's interesting — and why the device works — is that the volunteer feels in control of the choice. Of course, the reality is that the magician has offered the *illusion* of control, and that's precisely the key to the operation.

Naturally, as negotiators, we must always operate ethically and be mindful of the line between persuasion and manipulation. And we can lean into people's natural tendency to prefer control and provide choices as part of our negotiation process.

To the extent you can provide your counterpart a choice — particularly where the choice has high value to the other side and low cost to you — you're transferring value that, if you play your cards wisely, you can trade for a reciprocal negotiating gain.

And that trade — *voila!* — can help lead to a more satisfactory negotiation for all involved.

Can I Control It?

> *"In life our first job is this, to divide and distinguish things into two categories: externals I cannot control, but the choices I make with regard to them I do control. Where will I find good and bad? In me, in my choices."*
>
> *--Epictetus*

These words of Epictetus set forth an essential — if not *the most essential* — philosophical tenet of Stoicism. Separating those things we can control from what we cannot. Identifying what is worth trying to change, and what is futile. Focusing our efforts and attention on what we can do, in each present moment, to move closer to our goals.

Distinguishing uncontrollable externals from controlled choices just so happens to be a highly effective everyday negotiation skill, as well. For that reason, this theme recurs frequently in discussion of useful negotiating tools.

And it requires practice to train yourself to ask, in the face of a challenging dispute with a difficult adversary, these critical questions:

- *Is this something (or, someone) I can control?*

- *And, if not, how can I control my choices with respect to this immovable force and reach the best possible outcome?*

The Paradox of Control

> *"The more we value things outside our control, the less control we have."*
> —*Epictetus*

On a recent trip to a street market, my teenage son was shopping for a Mexican League soccer jersey. I, along with a good friend and his daughter accompanying us, watched patiently as the boy searched through a vendor's 10 or 15 hanging shirts of dazzling colors and varying sizes. Meanwhile, a grizzled storekeeper and his assistant continued to bring down shirt after shirt for my son to try. (Amazingly, they opined that he looked great in all of them.)

The bargaining began soon thereafter. We asked how much for a shirt; the storeman tried to entice us to buy multiple jerseys, quoting different prices in pesos depending on how many we'd purchase, and so on. The usual dance.

When decision time came, several pairs of eyes upon him, my son pulled me aside and whispered, "I don't know what to do. I'm feeling too much pressure!"

So I figured I'd help him by alleviating that pressure. "You know, we can always leave, see what other shirts are around the market, and come back later if you want. You don't have to get anything here."

"No," he said after a few seconds of thoughtful consideration. "After all of this, I'm not leaving here without a deal," he clarified firmly.

Sure enough, minutes later, we walked out with a sporty Club América shirt (at a slight discount), and my son was beaming from ear to ear.

We can take several negotiation lessons from this simple transaction, but to me one in particular stood out. When faced with the possibility of terminating the negotiations without a shirt in hand, my son realized quickly that his alternative — leaving shirtless and disappointed — was less attractive than bearing down and making a choice. His reaction to the walk-away option revealed that he would've paid even full freight to have a jersey, and "no deal" was no option at all.

As surrogate negotiator for my son on the shirt transaction, I found it extremely helpful to know that he wasn't willing to walk away. That knowledge provided important boundaries to guide the haggling in which one typically engages at the market.

However, it was also interesting how quickly providing a choice — suggesting the possibility of terminating negotiations — removed pressure from the process. At the same time, presenting the possibility of leaving empty-handed helped my son focus his priorities and move directly toward more productive, clear-headed decision-making.

As a mediator, I observe frequently that people respond much more positively to proposals when they don't feel forced into taking or leaving an offer. Some negotiators like to add arbitrary time constraints ("If you don't take it today by 5 p.m., the deal's off the table!"), couple offers with veiled threats ("If you won't accept, we'll file suit tomorrow!"), or use other pressure-building techniques designed to manipulate the other side. Most of the time, adding unnecessary pressure has the contrary effects of both turning off the decision-maker and aggravating the party's counsel.

When trying to persuade another party to agree with you, why make the party more uncomfortable or their decision even more difficult? It's a bit counterintuitive but, in practice, people really do respond better to being nudged, or pulled, as opposed to being *pushed* into a decision.

Granting your counterpart the freedom to decide grants a sense of control that, in many instances, can mean the difference between an unresolved dispute and a satisfactory resolution.

The Will is not the Way

"Let life ripen and then fall. Will is not the way at all."
— *Lao Tzu, from* The Way of Life According to Lao Tzu

We know that a fundamental tenet of Stoicism involves the separation of that which we can control from that over which we are powerless. That thing you're stressing over, worrying about, or dreading — can you control it, or is it out of your hands? If it is within your power to solve a problem or create a favorable result, then take action. However, if you are facing an obstacle over which you have no control, then let it go.

Lao Tzu, the ancient Chinese philosopher connected with Taoism, delivers a similar message. As much as we might want things to turn out a certain way, we can't always *will* them to happen as we'd choose. Instead of wishing it weren't raining, put on a raincoat. Or opt to stay inside. Stuck in a traffic jam? Turn on the radio, listen to a podcast, or call an old friend to catch up. If you think you can take a detour and avoid the congestion then, by all means, go for it.

But, of course, so many things are truly out of our control, and what remains for us is to respond and manage our options as best we can. It's a shame the traffic is so heavy, but what are you going to do? Gnashing your teeth, gripping the steering wheel, cursing at the car in front of you . . . none of that gets you anywhere.

The lesson of Lao Tzu can be useful to us in negotiation, as well. Sometimes, you're in conflict with someone who might be persuaded to see things your way. Or perhaps you're trying to unravel a problem with many facets that requires you to collaborate with another person, or perform extra work, or maybe do something else that can push you to your goal. If you can impact a result, you can choose your approach.

When you determine your obstacle is truly unmovable, and you have no power to control the result, reassess your options. True wisdom lies in knowing the difference between the controllable and the inevitable.

Uncovering Your Options

Often, when conducting a mediation, I talk with the parties about using negotiation as a way to uncover options. A prepared party enters mediation with a solid understanding of how the world *might* look if the case doesn't settle at mediation. That understanding should include each party's best and worst alternatives to settlement, along with a recognition that the future is inherently unpredictable.

Thus, when it comes time to mediate, the logical goal should be to uncover ranges of possible settlement values.

This goal is apt whenever we negotiate.

There is no winner or loser in negotiation. So it's not about beating your opponent. Entering a negotiation with a goal of winning, or not losing, just doesn't fit. Try thinking of negotiating to gain information, understanding, and a measure of control.

Once you negotiate to the point of reaching your most attractive settlement proposal, then – and only then – you can rationally compare the alternatives of settling versus not settling. It's really the same with any negotiation, where your rational decision must be comparing (a) the choice of agreeing on the terms available to (b) the alternative of an ongoing dispute.

That is, you negotiate to uncover your set of options, and those options inform your decision to agree or walk away.

Thus, it's critical to remain patient and *negotiate to the point of at least understanding the other party's best offer*. If you don't know what they're willing to offer – if you haven't uncovered all your options – how can you make an educated choice about your future?

Timing is Everything

We are experiencing higher than normal call volumes. Your call is important to us and will be answered in the order in which it was received . . .

"I've been on hold for 43 minutes now. This is the last thing I have time for. Ridiculous."

"So frustrating," I added, trying to ease the tension. "Do you think it would be better to call back next week, during regular business hours, so you don't waste any more time with this right now?"

Is This A Good Time To Talk?

It was a 2021 holiday weekend, around 9 p.m. My friend was waiting to talk with an airline's customer service department to negotiate a couple of details — items needing correction due to a prior company error — on a flight scheduled for months away. During that particular weekend, a winter storm was causing massive flight delays, and a COVID-19 surge had forced an overwhelming number of additional cancellations.

Not a good day to be flying. And not a good time to be dealing with an airline's customer service department unless you absolutely have to.

Consider: When the airline representative finally picks up, the conversation will be hamstrung from the start. The customer is coming into the call annoyed, because she's been waiting on the line nearly an hour, subjected to an endless loop of "on hold" jingles, airline ads, and robotic "apologies for the wait" explanations that ring hollow. Not the ideal way to treat your clients.

Many of the company representatives are undoubtedly highly skilled, good people, trying to do their best in tough situation. *Can you imagine a job where your core function is dealing with complaints, frustrations, and problems, many of which are completely out of your (and your company's) control?* (Some of you surely can!). And no matter who picks up the call — even if you draw the Customer Service Employee of the Month — we know a few things generally: It's a holiday weekend, it's the night shift, and global airline schedules are in chaos. We can only imagine the number of calls this rep is having to handle and the mix of angry, frustrated, and challenging customers he or she must be managing.

It's natural for customers to be frustrated by these situations. *Why don't they hire more people? Didn't they realize the call center would be busy tonight? Why do they need my email address again? Seriously? How can they not see my account information in the computer after I've entered it six times?*

But you can't control that stuff. It's going to happen. It's COVID, it's a snowstorm, it's an overworked company staff. Budgets have been slashed, cutbacks enforced. It's an endless series of faceless, upset customers. And it's a holiday weekend. Both the caller and the rep would probably rather be doing a million other things.

Nothing of this helps set you up for a productive conversation. Another customer in the queue, another underpaid, overworked rep in a call center headset.

What Can You Control?

In this scenario, though, what *can* you control? Of course, you can call back another day, at another time, after the storm has passed (literally and figuratively), and set yourself up with greater odds for success. Your matter is not urgent, albeit irritating, and it stands to reason that tackling your issue with clearer, calmer heads would be a positive step.

An important, often overlooked key to resolving disputes lies in timing. Before tackling the substance of a disagreement, think about how simply controlling *when* you have your conversation can impact your probability of attaining favorable results.

In this airline illustration, an obvious tack would be to revisit the conversation and call back in a calmer, less busy moment, when both sides can address your flight details free of duress and unnecessary pressure.

Controlling the timing of your difficult conversations, to the extent possible, can significantly impact your potential outcomes. The lesson from our airline anecdote, in a nutshell: If you need to negotiate changes to a far-off airplane ticket, don't do it when you and your customer service agent are under added stress. If you can, wait until skies are calm and extraneous pressure subsides.

The lesson impacts your approach to conflict resolution in a range of other personal and professional contexts.

Although various aspects of a negotiation and its milieu will be out of your control, you can often affect a negotiation's timing. Just as you realize that calling your airline's customer service department on a different day, at a different moment, can relieve certain pressures on your eventual discussion, you can choose *when* to have certain conversations.

Setting Yourself Up For Success

Optimizing your negotiation timing is an intuitive strategy that can be easy to overlook. I learned this lesson vividly years ago.

I was ready to ask a for a pay raise at my job, and after months of thinking about it I needed to approach my boss. Early one Monday morning, I happened to be in her office and, after having stewed over it intently during the prior weekend, figured I'd broach the raise. I assumed I'd mention it and then we'd schedule a chat.

"Oh, a raise, huh? Let's talk about it right now. I have a million things to do this week, and another meeting starting in 10 minutes. Actually, this whole month is going to be insane. But now's fine," she said impatiently.

Monday morning. *Strike one. Early* Monday morning. *Strike two.* My boss was very busy and under time constraints. *Strike three.* We were in her office, on her home turf, and I was not fully prepared. *Strike four.* Neither of us had even taken our morning coffee yet, which she habitually did at 10 a.m. *Well, I'm way out of strikes, and my list has only just begun.*

I made several critical errors in that raise conversation, and a category of them can be summed up with this: *timing.* An early Monday, before coffee, prior to full preparation, and in her busy office? The conversation itself was going to be difficult enough on its merits. The timing made everything that much harder.

Obviously, an opportunity for more pre-discussion preparation would've been ideal. But imagine how much different the feel of the same conversation would have been on a quiet, Friday afternoon, at the end of a productive week at the office. Better, right? Suppose my boss had just returned from an amazing vacation, refreshed, caught up, and in amazingly positive spirits. That, too, would present a favorable backdrop. Or what if instead of pre-coffee I'd initiated the conversation after lunch — or at lunch, even — the day after our team had successfully completed a major project? The setting, and set-up, of our talk would have been measurably different.

Helping Them To Help You

Naturally, you must know your audience and understand who's on the other side of your conversation. Some people are at their best first thing in the morning; others can barely function without that first jolt of caffeine. One colleague might be most approachable at the close of business; another is always in a harried rush out the door at 6 p.m. sharp. When your spouse or partner begins to wind down and relax at the end of a long day, is that an ideal moment to review your lengthy "to-do" list of home repair projects? (The answer, of course, depends on you, your mate, and your to-do list.)

Capitalizing on a conversation's timing depends on a range of skills, all of which contribute to your success as a negotiator. Empathy is important, so you can put yourself in the other person's shoes and envision how his or her reaction might vary with timing. Listening and observation skills will be critical, too, to help you gauge your counterpart's preferences and habits (*What time does he eat lunch, again? When was she coming back from that Caribbean cruise? When is my teen's big History exam?*), any number of which can factor into their receptiveness. As always, preparation is key.

A foundational Stoic principle teaches us that only certain things are within our control, and that we should focus our actions on those things. In a negotiation we can control only certain factors, as well, and must accept other immovable forces as they are.

Why not do everything possible to set the stage for a productive exchange? When you can influence the timing of a conversation, consider carefully how negotiating at an optimal moment would best position you for a favorable outcome.

A Worthwhile Distraction

"Therefore, the mind freed from passions is an impenetrable fortress — a person has no more secure place of refuge for all time."
—Marcus Aurelius

A recurring Stoic theme we discuss here is harnessing our emotional reactions. Keeping our cool. Resisting those emotional rushes that can override our rational brains and decision-making functions. Managing our passions and choosing to act, to the extent possible, from a place of calm and objectivity.

A basic question naturally arises: "How am I supposed to do that?!?"

We all have preferred methods for controlling our reactions, keeping calm, and grounding decisions in reason. Does deep breathing help you relax and stay under control? How about taking a walk, or other forms of exercise? Perhaps, when faced with conflict, you need to take a break and simply remove yourself from the volatile situation before you say something you'll regret or further enflame an already heated discussion.

Here's a practical tip to consider. Those of you who have spent time around kids will be familiar with the technique of distraction. When kids get stuck on something, and particularly when they are upset to the point of throwing a tantrum, it's nearly impossible to reason with them. Just imagine the little toddler, crying on the floor of the supermarket, pointing to the candy shelf in tears because Mommy or Daddy said, "No!" Or picture the preschoolers fighting over that single toy, the one in the bin that they both happen to need desperately at the very same moment, kicking and swinging while calling each other names.

You're not going to have a rational discussion with these little ones while they're out of control. They're angry, sad, upset, disappointed, and frustrated. And in that state you simply can't talk sense with them. So what do you do? You distract, of course.

It's easy to conjure up distraction techniques that might work in these situations. "You know, kids, there's another toy RIGHT HERE. Doesn't this look like fun?" Or, "Hey, buddy, can you help me find your favorite fruit in the grocery store? We can count the aisles until we get there." And so on.

In mediations, or other situations when people get "hung up" on something during conflict, you might consider a related technique. Instead of distraction, I often think of it as "redirection."

To nudge a person off a heated topic, when you sense the conversation is on the brink of becoming unproductive (or even worse — destructive), try to redirect, or refocus, towards objectivity. One basic way to do this is to take out a pen and paper, or something like a whiteboard if you're working virtually or digitally, and literally write out the numbers or terms underlying your disagreement. As a mediator, during a discussion break I might assign each party the "homework" of writing out their basic positions and interests. Sometimes it's helpful to set out, in written form, the different categories or components of an argument. Then all involved can see clearly the items upon which they agree and those remaining in dispute.

This little technique sounds very simple. It *is* very simple. But it works.

Redirecting focus from unsolvable arguments to tangible, practical action-items — things that can be more readily resolved and agreed-upon as part of a rational, fact-based conversation — both clarifies the discussion and gently moves the parties towards addressing those items they can actually control.

You can always return to the emotionally charged issues and address them as needed, and in an appropriate manner, of course. In the meantime, though, refocusing the conversation and engaging people's creative, problem-solving aptitudes can lay the groundwork for a productive solution.

Escapable Faults

It's silly to try to escape other people's faults. They are inescapable. Just try to escape your own."
—Marcus Aurelius

As a mediator, I frequently encounter parties that just plain don't like each other. Sometimes, they actually hate and can't stand to look at one another. Often, they can't bring themselves to speak directly and choose instead to communicate completely through me as a third-party intermediary.

"I've got nothing to say to her and don't want to hear it. She's rude, self-centered, and obnoxious," one litigant recently explained to me of an adversary.

"He's one of the worst people I've ever met, and his company never showed me an ounce of respect," another party told me of her ex-employer.

In our everyday lives, too, we encounter people who we think are flawed. Maybe you have a selfish uncle, rude landlord, or a former spouse in your life that gives you grief. We interact with strangers all of the time, too, and — let's face it — those encounters aren't all pleasant.

But what's the point of dwelling on others' imperfections? Even if you're completely correct, and that other person is detestable in every way, how does that help you in a negotiation setting? Does it bring you closer to your goal? How often have you been able to resolve a conflict by changing a person's nature or character?

In mediations, I try to help people see that focusing on others' faults (as they perceive them) is counter-productive.

Instead of wishing that the company rep was a better person, that your ex- wasn't so selfish, or that your opposition wasn't behaving so irrationally, refocus on how you react and respond. Remember, separating what we can control from what we cannot is a bedrock Stoic principal that can guide skilled negotiators.

As Marcus Aurelius reminds us, the only faults we have even a chance of escaping are our own.

PRINCIPLE THREE: OBJECTIVITY

Lacking an objective perspective can lead to prolonged disputes and prevent opposing sides from finding common ground towards resolutions. When you find yourself disagreeing with someone, or in the midst of a dispute, seek objectivity.

Is there an objectively right or wrong answer to the subject of your disagreement? Or is your dispute a matter of opinion, so that there's really no "right" or "wrong"?

When you're going in circles in a dispute, pause and question whether you're arguing about opinions or facts. If provable facts will settle the argument, let the search for objective truth be your guide. Although human decisions are often motivated by emotional responses, at least attempting to center a discussion on measurable facts will be your best path towards productive dialogue.

Beliefs are tricky because they are difficult to measure, prove, or disprove. People occasionally can believe opposite things and both be right. They can disagree on certain points but still find enough on which they can agree so that their dispute is resolvable and the conflict ultimately disappears.

At other times, though, when two people believe opposite things, they can both be wrong, in whole or in part, when neither side is 100% right.

There are at least two sides to every story. An objective viewpoint often yields insight beyond our reflexive, yes-or-no, black-and-white ways of thinking. Between greatly different and competing viewpoints, the "truth" – or, at least, a more objective solution – often lies somewhere in between. Frequently, accurate assessment of the most likely outcome will lie not in the blacks or whites, but in the shades of gray.

To the extent we can see situations objectively and without judgment, the more accurately we are perceiving things, and the better our decision-making.

This notion is very much in keeping with Stoic principles, and I've observed it play out favorably in countless negotiations. As a neutral mediator, I try to help people see the other side of the proverbial coin, so they can more accurately and objectively assess the facts and law underlying a case.

Frequently, and predictably, negotiators can become so focused on their own arguments that they lose objectivity. Unfortunately, lacking an objective perspective can lead to prolonged disputes and prevent opposing sides from finding common ground towards resolutions.

Sure, when we're deeply involved in disagreement, objectivity becomes elusive. Opposing parties (and their attorneys) in a lawsuit, squabbling siblings, negotiating businesses on either side of a deal, debating politicians — there are so many examples out there — can easily become entrenched in an "us" versus "them," "right" versus "wrong," mentality. When that happens, it's increasingly difficult to see the other side of the issue.

We lose perspective because we tend to see things in the light most favorable to our own point of view. We believe in our "truths" to the exclusion of other opinions or possibilities. This is precisely where mediators, for instance, can help people find common interests and opportunities for mutual gain, even when superficially they seem to be dug into incorrigible positions in conflict.

There is a "my-side" bias that creeps in – in conflict and

negotiation settings – that can keep us from properly assessing risk or fully appreciating the other side's perspective. It's easy to become entrenched in our own positions and then build and evaluate evidence in a manner slanted towards the way we see things. Cognitive errors like this, related to confirmation bias (*i.e.*, the tendency to over-value supporting evidence and devalue contrary evidence), can create barriers to resolution and lead to poor decisions.

On the other hand, Stoicism promotes clear, unbiased, logical thinking, and reason. If you view negotiations as a series of decisions we make – a useful perspective – you find that objectivity helps us see things as they are rather than through rose-colored glasses. Stoicism places a high value on being reasonable as a path to contentment, finding the truth, and living a good life.

Epictetus spoke of rationality and the importance of seeking to get to what is actually true. Taking an objective approach incorporates all sides of a challenge, problem, or conflict, helps you identify your blindspots, and also allows you to figure out what the other side needs to create an agreement opportunity.

Accepting things as they actually are – and then focusing on how you can move forward by acting on what's directly in front of you – generates resiliency, which is immeasurably valuable to negotiators.

Striving for objectivity also helps you see clearly your best and worst alternatives to not reaching an agreement. Stoicism leads us to a couple of concepts that help here:

- *premeditatio malorum* – method of visualizing the worst-case scenario for any situation, so we can be prepared and then mitigate what we might face; and

- *momento mori* – reminding yourself that we're all going to die, so that we can appreciate the current moment.

The concept of identifying your worst-case scenario will remind negotiation students of the familiar "worst alternative to a negotiated agreement" (WATNA). *If we can't reach a resolution, how bad are my options?*

Thorough negotiators make informed decisions only in comparison to their WATNA and, its conceptual cousin, best alternative to a negotiated agreement (BATNA). Mapping your range of alternatives, and evaluating them with reference to a potential agreement you might negotiate, provides a foundation for quality, objective decision-making.

Objectivity: What You Can Do, Starting Now

As a starting point: Focusing on the deal, or the conflict, rather than an "us versus them" mentality, can reduce emotional reaction and help mold a more collaborative conversation.

Next, is there an objectively right or wrong answer to the subject of your disagreement? Or is your dispute a matter of opinion, so that there's really no "right" or "wrong"?

Whenever you can find objective facts and data to shed light on a dispute, seek them out. Although it can be difficult to change a person's view of what is "true," especially with respect to closely held beliefs, it's virtually impossible to change someone's subjective opinion. If your friend Sheri doesn't like strawberries, you can't convince her that, no, she actually does. Sheri doesn't have to enjoy strawberries, as delicious as they are to you, and you don't have to like Sheri's preferred raspberries. There's just no right or wrong there.

However, where a disagreement can be settled with reference to something objective, like data and factual information, use those to gain common ground. Instead of arguing with a potential buyer about the fair sale price of your house, can you locate a comparable property (a "comp") or other relevant fact-based evidence that answers your question within a reasonable range? Did you meet specific criteria established to evaluate your work performance, so you can demonstrate to your boss your entitlement to a raise, instead of expressing a mere opinion of your worth to the company and throwing out a number *you* like? Even if you can't persuade Sheri to like strawberries, you can still prove that a strawberry is *not* a raspberry.

The same mental models I use as a professional mediator are highly useful tools to manage conflict and drive negotiations. Fortunately, we can all gain access to some of the neutral postures that mediators – objective, neutral parties – can bring to a discussion. Mediators are trained to listen to all sides of a dispute, allow the parties to express themselves and hear each other, and guide communications in a way that ameliorates the emotional sting one or more sides might be experiencing. The end result, ideally, is productive idea exchange and thoughtful negotiation.

In less formal settings, as well as in our personal lives, it pays to engage what I call your "inner mediator" and seek out objective perspectives. Tapping into your *inner mediator*, this mindset, entails approaching a situation objectively, and neutrally, and responding to facts instead of being driven by emotional reactions.

No, this is not easy, but seeing things objectively leads to greater clarity, understanding, and increased chance of reaching resolution. You'll need to train yourself, and it might take a lifetime of practice to develop this skill and habit to its fullest.

Luckily, though, there are a few things you can do today to start exercising your "objectivity" muscle. Try starting with these exercises to engage your inner mediator:

- Marcus Aurelius practiced "taking the view from above." This helps us get perspective and reminds us how small we are. So take a deep breath and step back. Look at your disagreement from the 30,000-foot view. How does it appear now? Does a broader perspective allow you to rethink or reprioritize what had previously seemed more or less important?

- Pretend, for a moment, that you are in your adversary's shoes. Perhaps you've even been there before under different circumstances. How would you argue for his or her position?

- If you were to tell your side of a story to a neutral party — a judge, another friend, a counselor, or maybe a family member — how would it sound? Can you imagine how the neutral would perceive the two (or more) sides to your dispute?

- Ask your counterpart to state what he or she believes to be your argument. This mere exercise — restating your position — will help shift that other person to a more objective viewpoint.

- If a friend or colleague were involved in the dispute in which you find yourself, what advice would you give? Seeing the situation from the outside can help you view things more clearly and objectively.

- Objectivity allows you to use techniques like "steelmanning," which gains you credibility and persuasiveness. Setting up the strongest version of your adversary's argument and persuading against that, rather than an exaggerated or misrepresented version of their position (as one might using a less savory "strawmanning" tactic), earns trust and believability.

Reactive Devaluation: Don't Lead Yourself Astray

At a recent mediation, I was faced with a familiar dilemma: *Why is this person rejecting the settlement offer on the table?*

I've come to expect the unexpected in settlement mediations. After all the years I've been working with disputing parties seeking to negotiate resolutions to their lawsuits, nothing really surprises me anymore.

But this one was initially puzzling. The person rejecting the proposed settlement offer was injured in an accident, and the defendant's insurer was offering to resolve her case for a substantial sum. The injured woman's attorney had opined that the settlement offer was reasonable under the circumstances. The defense attorney had advised her insurance client to pay more than it had initially intended, and they were willing to stretch in an effort to compromise and eliminate future risk.

The attorneys on both sides of the case viewed the settlement proposal as reasonable. As a neutral party, I generally don't judge what people will and will not accept to settle cases. In this instance, for what it's worth, I saw nothing objectively unreasonable about the pending offer.

Now, here's the interesting part: The offered settlement consisted of precisely what the plaintiff had stated, just an hour previously to her attorney and me privately, that she would accept. *It was what she wanted.* In fact, she had been adamant that if the insurer did *not* offer that amount — earlier in negotiations they were offering significantly less — she would walk away and never engage in future settlement discussions.

So there we were, with the plaintiff's "wish list" offer on the table, and she refused to accept it. *But why?*

Upon reflection, the answer was simple: reactive devaluation.

Separating The Subject From The Source

Reactive devaluation occurs when we resist ideas simply because they come from what (or whom) we perceive to be a negative source. When this common cognitive bias takes hold, one party devalues a counterpart's proposal because he or she doesn't like the counterpart or otherwise views the counterpart suspiciously.

That is, we reject an "enemy" proposal based not on its merits but, rather, on its origin. If we're not careful, our views of the opposing party can cloud our judgment, such that we can misinterpret and fail to assess accurately substantive negotiation offerings.

Reactive devaluation can prevent parties' agreements because of how they view each other, even causing them to pass up objectively good deals. Parties battling in the courtroom are active participants in an adversarial system, so it's natural for them to discredit each other's arguments. In negotiation, though, an effective process depends on the parties trusting each other, at least somewhat, and working together.

In my mediation involving the injured woman and the insurance company, for example, the plaintiff soured on the potential settlement terms as soon as they came from the opposing party. To put it plainly, the plaintiff liked the deal but despised the source of the proposal (*i.e.*, the defendant insurance company). Her dislike of the insurer was so strong that it prevented her from seeing the company's offer as fair or reasonable, even though she herself had previously blessed the precise deal terms that the offer encompassed.

Missed Negotiation Opportunities

As soon as the plaintiff perceived the deal terms as coming from the opposing party, her evaluation of the deal's merits completely changed.

There are various psychological factors that leave us susceptible to reactive devaluation in the negotiation setting. A lack of trust, overly adversarial or antagonistic attitude, or even animosity between negotiating parties can inhibit the parties' ability to evaluate proposals dispassionately. The end result is that all involved miss out on real opportunities; no one wins, but everyone loses.

Of course, you don't have to look far in our daily lives to see reactive devaluation tendencies in action. Whenever people drift into an "us versus them" mentality — routing for different sports teams, working for business competitors, pledging unquestioned allegiance to a political party, or otherwise identifying strongly with opposing groups — be on the lookout for reactive devaluation.

Can all *of your adversary's ideas be half-baked, or might some of them be reasonable and worthy of consideration? How is it possible that every single idea from that* other *group is completely and totally bonkers in the eyes of the opposing side (and vice versa)? Why is it that every teenager on Earth rejects anything and everything his or her parents say? (They can't possibly* all *be bad suggestions, right?)*

Luckily, there are negotiation strategies you can employ when you suspect reactive devaluation is impacting your decision-making process. Let's take a closer look.

First, a brief review. So we've introduced *reactive devaluation*: our tendency to resist ideas simply because they come from a perceived negative source. This common cognitive bias can cause a perfectly rational person — like the injured woman at the negotiating table we met earlier — to make irrational negotiation decisions.

You don't want to be one of those people. Because people who don't recognize biases like these can, quite simply, miss out on legitimate opportunities.

As you'll recall, the injured woman initially rejected a reasonable settlement offer that she would have accepted were it not for the source of the offer: the insurance company defendant, whom the woman strongly disliked. *[Side note: By the end of a challenging mediation process, the woman realized the true value of the offer and ultimately decided to resolve her case.]*

Was the woman *right* to mistrust the insurance company? Was she *wrong* to reject the insurer's settlement offer at first, and then *right* later to reconsider?

For our purposes, none of that matters. The issue is that the woman reflexively rejected the offer based not on its merits but, rather, on its source. She nearly missed an opportunity to make a sound decision, accept a proposal that met her needs, and resolve a dispute — all because she devalued the offer owing to her views of the offeror.

Why Reactive Devaluation Matters

You can probably think of many everyday situations — at home, at work, or out and about in your daily life — in which an unfavorable view of the other side keeps us from honestly evaluating a particular proposal. Perhaps you've noticed that we live in such polarized times that, routinely, ideas are described simultaneously "the best!" and "the worst!", depending on who's describing and who's proposing. How can that possibly be?

Or maybe you're familiar with that routine in which your two teenagers need to agree on a place for dinner, and each rejects the other's suggestion simply because *the other guy* offered it up — so that each effectively would rather starve than "give in" and accept the other's perfectly delicious idea? I imagine you can relate to this or a similar scenario.

When reactive devaluation kicks in, it can cloud our ability to see the true value of proposals apart from their source. We don't want that to happen to us. Furthermore, we don't want someone else to reject *our* valid negotiation proposals because of a reactive devaluation effect.

How To Counteract Reactive Devaluation

Is it easy to overcome reactive devaluation? Of course not. That's the bad news.

The good news: Like so many other cognitive biases and fallacies (sunk cost fallacy, loss aversion, or confirmation bias, to name just a few), if we can't avoid these traps perhaps we can at least contain them.

A few things to think about when you assess a proposal and sense that emotions, in the context of a negotiation, dispute, or conflict, could be hampering objective evaluation:

- The first step, to which we just alluded, is recognition. Just like we don't like to think we're capable of being fooled by our own minds and most of us swear we're better than average drivers (no, that math doesn't work!), we must realize we can make errors in judgment. Humility is a key trait of strong negotiators, and that allows them room to learn from their counterparts and recognize their own fallibilities. Reactive devaluation is natural, and we can anticipate it in negotiation settings.

- Try to be as objective as possible. Take a step back, gain perspective, and engage your "inner mediator." This can help give you a clearer, more dispassionate look at your situation and negotiation options. *How would things appear to you if you were not emotionally involved, or if someone else (i.e., someone who did not enflame, anger, or upset you) had presented the proposal you're weighing?*

- Consider how you would advise a friend or family member were that person in your situation. Sometimes that mental exercise — imagining yourself in the role of advisor — allows you to gain that elusive, more neutral perspective you need to execute thoughtful decisions at the negotiation table. *If you would tell your hypothetical advisee to take the deal or make the offer, why would you, yourself, behave any differently?*

- You might also consider enlisting the help of a friend, colleague, family member, or other person suitable to act as a "neutral" to guide your negotiation efforts. One reason that mediation — utilizing a mediator as a neutral, third party negotiation facilitator — helps legal disputants resolve their differences is that it lessens the sting of reactive devaluation. Parties to a conflict can become so focused on beating the opponent that they find it difficult to shift to more creative, problem-solving modes. However, the same proposal one party would reject coming from the opposition might become suddenly palatable were it to come from a neutral party, like a mediator or someone serving a similar role.

- Suppose you're negotiating against or in conflict with someone you suspect could be hampered by reactive devaluation. You want that person to see your reasonable proposal for what it is, objectively, and not reject the proposal simply because it was "yours."

One technique you can try is extending an offer that includes a choice or choices. (A classic parents know: "Hey, kids, would you like to start with your broccoli or your spinach? The choice is yours!") Making a choice often gives people a feeling of power and control that could otherwise be threatened by accepting *someone else's* solution.

- Finally, a reactive devaluation-defusing tool for our top negotiation students. This one is particularly challenging, but I have seen it utilized in negotiations and assure you can succeed: Present your proposal in a manner in which *the other person feels it is his or her own*. As forerunner of modern probability theory (and lots more) Blaise Pascal put it, "People are generally better persuaded by the reasons which they have themselves discovered than by those which have come into the mind of others."

- That is, the best persuader of a person is ... that person. If you can become skilled enough to float a negotiation idea in a way that so artfully and directly addresses the other person's needs, you can conceivably both remove the specter of reactive devaluation and also guide the person towards a shared, mutually beneficial outcome. (Have you tried experimenting with the Socratic method,[3] for example?) In the end, your counterpart will have the space to conclude that the offered proposal is valid *and* persuasive — after all, it was the counterpart's own idea, right? — and worthy of full consideration.

Final Takeaways: Reactive Devaluation

- Recognize that reactive devaluation exists. It's a real, natural phenomenon, and it creeps into decisions we make every day.

- The next time you find yourself reacting negatively to a concept someone else proposes, stop and consider if your reaction is to the person or the underlying idea.

- When you encounter potential effects of this common cognitive bias, take steps to minimize its impact on your negotiation process.

Finding Your "Inner Mediator"

In Search Of Objectivity

Attorneys on either side of a lawsuit, under our adversarial legal system, oppose each other in the courtroom. One attorney argues for her client's interests, and the opposing counsel argues on behalf of his client. The judge and jury hear the evidence, consider the arguments of the plaintiff and defendant, and render a decision.

Arbitration and mediation are alternatives to traditional courtroom processes that can provide enhanced efficiency and flexibility. Instead of going to court, parties can present their case to an arbitrator, who acts as a private judge in a more informal proceeding. At mediation, parties engage in structured negotiations, led by a neutral, third party — the mediator — and seek to resolve their dispute by mutual agreement.

Here's the thing: If people could resolve these matters among themselves, they wouldn't need to turn to third parties. Sometimes, of course, parties in conflict are able to communicate, negotiate, and problem-solve in lieu of seeking outside assistance. Often, because neutrals are trained specifically to resolve disputes — and because conflict can be incredibly challenging — trials, arbitration hearings, and mediations are the conflict solutions litigants ultimately need.

Why are these neutral, third parties so valuable when it comes to resolving disputes? For one (very important!) thing, judges, arbitrators, and mediators all bring *objectivity*.

Gaining Perspective

When we're deeply involved in disagreement, objectivity becomes elusive. Opposing parties (and their attorneys) in a lawsuit, squabbling siblings, negotiating businesses on either side of a deal, debating politicians — there are so many examples out there — can easily become entrenched in an "us versus them," "right against wrong," mentality. When that happens, it's increasingly difficult to see the other side of the issue.

We lose perspective because we tend to perceive the world in the light most favorable to our own point of view. We believe in our "truths" to the exclusion of other opinions or possibilities. This is precisely where mediators, in particular, come in. Mediators help people find common interests and opportunities for mutual gain, even when superficially they seem to be dug into incorrigible, conflicting positions.

Luckily, we can all gain access to some of the neutral postures that mediators bring to a discussion.

No, this is not easy, but seeing things objectively leads to greater clarity, understanding and, ideally, resolution. You'll need to train yourself, and it might take a lifetime of practice to develop this skill and habit to its fullest.

Engaging Your "Inner Mediator"

Luckily, though, there are a few things you can do today to start exercising your "objectivity" muscle. Try revisiting these hacks to engage your "inner mediator":

- Take a deep breath and step back. Look at your disagreement from the 30,000-foot view. How does it appear now?

- Pretend, for a moment, that you are in your adversary's shoes. Perhaps you've even been there before under different circumstances. How would you argue for his or her position?

- If you were to tell your side of a story to a neutral party — a judge, another friend, a counselor, or maybe a family member — how would it be perceived? Can you imagine how the two (or more) sides to your dispute would sound to the neutral listener?

- If a friend or colleague were involved in the dispute in which you find yourself, what advice would you give?

Choosing Sides

If you were to ask a room of experts for their number one, absolute, top negotiation tip, my bet is that it would be nearly unanimously this: Prepare.

But it's not that simple. Today we examine a reason why.

Preparation: Negotiation's Non-Negotiable

To be most successful as a negotiator, you simply must prepare. Sure, sometimes you can wing it and come out okay. You'll inevitably find yourself in less-than-ideal situations and have to negotiate on the fly. Believe me, I see attorneys enter mediation unprepared more than you'd think — so much that I even wrote a "survival guide" book[4] to help attorneys survive (and even excel) when thrust into less-than-ideal negotiation scenarios.

But there is no substitute for smart, thorough negotiation preparation. Of course, we can debate the best ways to prepare to negotiate. I've certainly been privy to the processes of negotiators who prepare much more thoroughly than others. You find a style that works best for you. But the need to prepare is, well, non-negotiable.

I mediated a case recently that nonetheless started me thinking: Can we *over-prepare* for a negotiation?

Negotiation Example: Too Much Of A Good Thing?

The case at hand involved both factual and legal disputes.

The parties had different versions of the events that lead to the lawsuit, and the attorneys had crafted complex arguments to support their respective legal positions.

One of the lawyers presented a particularly impassioned opening statement — which was interesting, given that there are no juries to sway at mediation — that eloquently outlined all of the reasons why their legal interpretation was correct. As the attorney spoke, her client nodded approvingly and occasionally flashed a satisfied grin.

Once I separated the parties into private rooms to conduct further negotiations, the presentation continued. And it continued, for nearly an hour, with great fervor.

It occurred to me that the more this attorney spoke, the more she and her client seemed to be digging into their positions. Their energies fed off one another, and by the time we finished our first private meeting they were practically ready to sprint into the courtroom and launch the greatest trial our jurisdiction had ever seen.

Clearly, this group had prepared. They had gathered their facts, researched every corner of the legal landscape, and came primed to set the record straight.

Unfortunately, there's no "record" at mediation. No judge, no jury. There's no winner, and no loser. No right, no wrong. Mediation is about structured negotiation, collaboration, patience, creativity, and problem-solving.

In this case, reminiscent of others I encounter from time to time, the one party and its counsel had effectively prepared themselves into *thinking they just couldn't lose*.

If I've learned anything from mediating and dealing with thousands of cases over the years, it's that there's no sure thing. Just as soon as you think you have all the facts on your side, and the law going your way, there's a surprise. Something you didn't see coming, or someone else who tells a completely different story, or a judge or jury who simply isn't persuaded by your side.

So I pondered this — can you be *too* prepared entering a negotiation? — and was reminded of an interesting phenomenon: *myside bias*.

The Rose-Colored Negotiation Lens: Myside Bias

It would be near heresy for me to suggest that you can over-prepare for a negotiation. You should absolutely know everything possible about your facts, any controlling authority, and basis for your opinions and positions. Do your research, set your goals, and figure out where your leverage is. And this goes for negotiations in both personal and business arenas.

However, also recognize that we're likely to see our own positions and views through the rose-colored lens of what's known as *myside bias*.[5] The more you gather your evidence, argue your point, and gear up for verbal sparring matches — I strongly suspect — you'll be increasingly susceptible to cementing your opinions to the exclusion of other viewpoints.

As with other cognitive biases that can mislead our decision-making, including confirmation bias, the sunk cost fallacy, and even the "I'm not biased" bias, among many others, awareness is the first step.

Myside bias, related to confirmation bias, refers to our tendency to evaluate evidence in a manner biased toward our own opinions. That is, we process information and interpret evidence selectively, in a way tending to support our own — and refute opposing — beliefs, opinions, and attitudes.

We're quick to spot the weaknesses in what the other side presents. And we're apt to downplay the weaker points, and focus on the strengths, of our own positions.

Stick with me here. In other words — you got it — *we're biased in recognizing our own biases*. And we're highly prone to this form of metacognitive bias or, for lack of a better term, incomplete self-awareness.

If we see things in a manner biased towards our own position entering a negotiation, then, how can we see things objectively? If we can't, how do we accurately assess risk and make sound decisions? Can we acknowledge the other side and the possibility that we could be missing something, or actually even be wrong?

Here are a few concepts you can take into your next negotiation or attempt to resolve conflict. Prepare for the encounter, advocate for your (or your clients') interests, aim to achieve realistic goals, and be ready to act assertively. Still, whether it's a multi-million dollar business deal or spat with your teenager, or anything in between, these ideas help you check your assumptions and counteract our "myside" tendencies:

- **Seek out objectivity**. Is there an objectively right or wrong answer to the subject of your disagreement? Or is your dispute a matter of opinion, such that neither side is correct or incorrect, and both viewpoints are worthy of consideration? After gathering your facts and preparing your arguments, can you still see the flip side of the coin? Can you empathize with your counterpart and at least understand the contentions opposing your own?

- **Stay humble**. Humble negotiators benefit from being open-minded and have a knack for seeing both the strengths and weaknesses of their positions. With humility comes greater objectivity and a more realistic assessment of risks. Recognizing the role luck and pure chance play in our lives, and appreciating that there can exist great value in perspectives that differ from our own, those that negotiate from a place of humility are better equipped to collaborate and make prudent decisions than those who lack empathy and fail to acknowledge the uncontrollable.

- **Critically question your thinking**. When faced with a strong counterargument, instead of simply trying to poke holes in that argument, consider whether you could have missed something or even made a mistake. Listen to the other side and stay curious. Ask why you're seeing things differently. Aim to learn more. Seek out, as best you can, the "truth" underlying your dispute.

- **Recognize and account for your emotions**. Remember that reactive devaluation concept we've discussed?[6] It can cause us to reject opposing offers and ideas based on their source rather than on their merits. Might your counterpart's position in your dispute be reasonable, even though you, in an adversarial posture, are unable to see that in the heat of disagreement? We are apt to react emotionally under these circumstances, and our reactions can inhibit our ability to analyze all sides objectively.

- **Beware of your blind spots**. Finally, as part of your pre-negotiation preparation, anticipate the other side's arguments and positions. What might you be missing on your end of the dispute? How would you defend opposing interests if you were sitting across the table?

The Opposite

One of *Seinfeld* TV-series character George Costanza's most memorable endeavors was his attempt, in famous episode, "The Opposite," to do the opposite of his every natural tendency. Lamenting his undeniable pattern of poor life choices and unsatisfying results, George's pal Jerry urged him to change his hard-luck ways using this logic: "If every instinct you have is wrong, then the opposite would have to be right."

A variant of George's "do the opposite" approach can be a useful tool in negotiation and mediation settings, too. How? It can help you combat common cognitive biases that infect our sound analysis and thinking, and thus allow you to become a more effective negotiator.

Considering the opposite of your negotiation position helps fight the common tendency to overvalue our own viewpoints and undervalue opposing views. Labels such as "confirmation bias" and the "ostrich effect," among others, can be used to describe our predispositions to listen to only the information that confirms our positions and to disregard negative or conflicting information. As *Thinking, Fast and Slow*[7] researchers Kahneman and Tversky have comprehensively described, we seek out and selectively interpret information in a manner that confirms our beliefs, and we proverbially stick our heads in the sand and pretend that potentially damaging information does not exist.

Effective negotiators thoroughly understand their best and worst alternatives to negotiated agreements. To reach that understanding they must be able to view their disputes objectively and appreciate both the positive and negative aspects of their bargaining positions. A "devil's advocate" exercise – essentially, arguing the other side of your case – helps us move beyond a propensity to misjudge the relative weight of our side's strengths and weaknesses.

Instead of allowing ourselves to dig in to our positions at the expense of considering other information and probabilities, and using George Costanza's "do the opposite" as a guide, we can view our dispute from perspectives other than our own. This enables us to empathize with our counterparts, giving us a better understanding of why they think and feel as they do, which is critical to effective dispute resolution.

If you are able to see the opposite side of your disagreement, negotiation, mediation, or other dispute, you will ultimately gain a more realistic, balanced assessment of your position. Such an assessment will help stave off overconfidence, a frequent byproduct of cognitive biases, that can leave you vulnerable to negotiating counter-attacks and -strategies.

In your next negotiation, take a cue from George Costanza. In appreciating the opposing side you will gain a useful tool to sharpen your arguments, anticipate and defuse contrary arguments, and negotiate with greater success.

Loss Aversion and Errors in Judgment

Suppose you're offered a bet based on a single coin flip: If it's tails, you lose $100. Now, to make this gamble worthwhile, how much would you have to stand to gain if the coin were to come up heads?

Think about it for a few seconds.

According to studies of renowned behavioral scientists Daniel Kahneman and Amos Tversky, noted for their scholarship related to cognitive biases, most people would require at least $200 for a winning flip. But why? If the odds of winning or losing a coin toss are 50-50, why wouldn't we accept the possibility of winning $101, or $150?

The answer is rooted in our tendency towards loss aversion and the prospect theory Kahneman and Tversky developed.[8] Their research suggests that *most people feel the sting of loss more intensely than the satisfaction of gain*, so that they'd require the possibility of winning $200 to offset potentially losing $100.

So why wouldn't we rationally accept a coin-flip wager where a loss would cost us $100 but a win would give us $101 or $150? In short, we hate losing more than we like winning. That is, it's better to *not lose* $100 than to win $100.

This concept, called loss aversion, is an important psychological principle that skilled negotiators can use to their advantage. On the flip side (yes, a pun), if you're not careful, loss aversion can cause us to fall for sunk cost and similar logical fallacies that lead to suboptimal decision-making.

The bias of loss aversion can impact our negotiations in

various ways. For example, is it rational to refuse a negotiated offer – say, a dollar amount to settle a lawsuit – because, though not a bad deal, it is below your stated "bottom line" and you can't bear taking a "loss"? Surely not. You might find it difficult to walk away from a suit unless you receive an offer with a *significantly* higher expected value, even though your reluctance could mean making an illogical decision and leaving money on the table.

We hate to lose more than we like to win.

How would you feel about selling a stock or, say, your house, for less than what you paid, even if the proposed deal reflects current market conditions and an objectively reasonable offer? And have you ever noticed that it's harder to give up a product or service after using it for a trial period? If so, your instinct to keep the product might be driven largely by your desire to avoid a loss.

Most every negotiation decision involves a trade-off: Each side has to give up something to get something else. Thus, the extent to which a proposal is framed as an avoidance of loss, or rather as a potential gain, can greatly influence how it is perceived and evaluated.

The Message or the Messenger?

Last week, I was preparing for what I anticipated would be a torturously difficult negotiation. The parties would be dug in and reluctant to compromise. They had virtually equally bargaining power, were smart and persistent, and could push each other's hot-buttons with brutal precision. Maintaining an ongoing relationship and striking a deal were obligatory, and time was of the essence.

It was Friday evening, and that meant our twin teenagers needed to agree on a restaurant for our weekly family dinner pick-up.

Predictably, as our discussion began, each kid's suggestion was unceremoniously rejected by the other guy. Sometimes, the rejection would come with a rationale; other times, it was a flat, "nope." And around we went, all involved growing hungrier and more frustrated by the minute.

Not surprisingly, each budding negotiator was refusing to go to places he'd have gladly gone were it not for the source of the proposal. Teenager #1 won't eat at this restaurant because the other one wants to, Teenager #2 won't go to that restaurant just because his counterpart named it, and so on. As we observed, my wife and I knew that all of the options would've been perfectly fine for the entire group. Deep down, surely the kids knew that, too. (Yes, we eventually found a compromise, which the parents proposed.)

Our tendency to resist ideas simply because they come from what we perceive to be a negative source is so common that psychology has a fancy name for this form of cognitive bias: reactive devaluation. (We've discussed this phenomenon before!) In a reactive devaluation scenario, someone devalues a counterpart's proposal because he or she doesn't like the counterpart or otherwise views the counterpart negatively.

Reactive devaluation can prevent parties' agreements because of how they view each other, even causing them to pass up objectively good deals. In our simple example with dinner selection, perfectly reasonable restaurant options – with which each diner would've independently been content – are eliminated because neither party wants to give in to the other. The end result is that all involved miss out on real opportunities; no one wins, but everyone loses.

You can probably think of many everyday situations – at home, at work, or out and about in your daily life – in which an unfavorable view of the other side keeps us from honestly evaluating a particular proposal. Perhaps you've noticed that we live in such polarized times that, routinely, ideas are described simultaneously "the best!" and "the worst!", depending on who's describing and who's proposing. How can that possibly be?

When reactive devaluation kicks in, it can cloud our ability to see the true value of proposals apart from their source.

One reason that mediation helps parties in legal disputes resolve their differences is that it lessens the sting of reactive devaluation. Parties to a conflict can become so focused on beating the opponent that they find it difficult to shift to more creative, problem-solving modes. The same proposal one party would reject coming from the opposition might become suddenly palatable were it to originate from a neutral party, like a mediator. Good mediators can inoculate ideas against attack by delivering and reframing them in an objective way. *Really good* mediators can even guide parties to arrive at agreement with each feeling like the resolution was its own idea.

For now, recognize that reactive devaluation exists. It's a real, natural phenomenon, and it creeps into decisions we make every day. Then the next time you find yourself reacting negatively to a concept someone else proposes, stop and consider if your reaction is to the person or the underlying idea.

If you can habitually evaluate from a more neutral perspective, might your decision-making change for the better?

PRINCIPLE FOUR: HUMILITY

Humility is an under-the-radar secret weapon of some of the absolute best negotiators and problem-solvers. Humble negotiators – those who recognize that they don't necessarily know everything about a dispute and could learn from the opposing view – benefit from being open-minded and have a knack for seeing both the strengths and weaknesses of their positions.

Increasingly, cognitive psychologists seem to appreciate the impact of humility — and the lack thereof — in any number of contexts. Knowing what we know, as well as what we *don't know*, helps us define the limits of our expertise in professional *and personal* endeavors.

Strong negotiators enter negotiations willing to test their assumptions, challenge their own beliefs, and adjust expectations based on what they might learn from their counterparts. Doing so allows negotiators to gain a more objective – and more accurate – assessment of all facets of their disputes or negotiating parameters.

I've observed these traits over the years, but only fairly recently have I been able to pinpoint humility as a root of these negotiators' successes.

With humility comes greater objectivity and a more realistic assessment of risks.

Those that negotiate from a place of humility recognize the role luck and pure chance play in our lives. They appreciate that there can exist great value in perspectives that differ from our own. What's more, humble negotiators are better equipped to collaborate and make prudent decisions than those who lack empathy and fail to acknowledge the uncontrollable.

People are so likely to overestimate their abilities – and underestimate their shortcomings – that this state of our condition has been given a name: the Dunning-Kruger effect. For the same reasons three-quarters of drivers might rate themselves as above-average[9] (obviously, this would be impossible!), we're generally not as good as we think we are at predicting the future or viewing ourselves objectively.

However, humble people tend to be curious, seeking that elusive objective viewpoint, and more at peace with uncertainty. In my experience, strong negotiators share these traits. They're interested in how their negotiating partners see the world, realize that there are two sides to every coin, and know that we're notoriously inaccurate in projecting the future.

The humble understand that there is more than one side to every story. They realize that between greatly different and competing viewpoints, the "truth" – or, at least, a more objective solution – often lies somewhere between, in the shades of gray.

If you've ever paid much attention to hurricane projection models, or forecasted rain chances, you know that even with the most advanced technology meteorologists can't precisely predict where these storms will go. And with a 10% rain chance, you can still find yourself drenched by an unlikely, yet very real – and very wet – scattered shower.

Although the limits of weather prediction make forecasters easy targets for skeptics – as the person who happens to get soaked by an unlikely passing thunderstorm – consider that we're all wandering through life like the forecasters. We can have a general sense of how the future will unfold, but a lot of what we see we must extrapolate, make our best guesses, and complete our predictive vision.

And our guesses are most likely cobbled together by much flimsier data than what's available to the highly-trained folks paid to predict the weather.

So how is this relevant to negotiation?

The humble negotiator acknowledges that one of the greatest obstacles to compromise and agreement is our inability to reckon with life's inherent unpredictability. When at the beginning of a mediation I ask both sides how they feel about their lawsuit, and they each tell me they have a 90% chance of winning, how can they both be right? What variables are involved in their predictions, and what assumptions are they making that may or may not be accurate? Is each side really viewing its case objectively?

These ideas, of course, come into play during most disagreements and disputes. It's human nature to seek certainty and predictability, and it's easier to see things as binary (yes/no, bad/good, rain/sunshine, etc.) than along a spectrum of possibility.

Once you start letting your ego guide your negotiations, you're in trouble. This is where I see a lot of problems come in for negotiators. If you're driven by emotions, you can lose the forest for the trees and miss the big picture.

Instead of asking ourselves why the weather forecasters always seem to get it wrong, it might be more useful to realize that we're all operating in a world of incredible variability and uncertainty.

The Stoics understood humility. They were not driven by ego or self-importance. They contemplated the impermanence of things, appreciating how short life is, and those realizations actually led them to focus on living good lives.

Marcus Aurelius was at one time the most powerful person in the world, as ruler of the Roman Empire. Nonetheless, he stressed the importance of the common good and being willing to learn from anyone, regardless of their relative powerlessness or station in life.

It takes courage (a Stoic virtue, incidentally) to accept that you don't have all the answers, to be able to acknowledge that and be willing to learn from your counterpart. But that ability opens up endless collaboration opportunities.

And it can be an absolute power move to admit you don't know something. How does that serve us?

- This display of humility opens the door for us to use our listening skills, which all polished negotiators know to be among their most critical tools for negotiation and persuasion.

- By being open to other perspectives, you collect valuable information and unlock creative problem-solving opportunities.

- You gain credibility and can earn the other side's trust. *Hey, this person is upfront and confident enough to acknowledge what he or she doesn't know.* Then, when you make another point with conviction, the other side understands that you mean it and *do* know what you're talking about.

And the good news is that you can begin to cultivate a more humble approach to negotiations. Sure, there's no definitive formula to resolving conflict. People are different, situations vary, and there's no one-size-fits-all approach that guarantees success. Sometimes, you can do absolutely everything correctly in managing a dispute and still wind up with a prolonged disagreement or deadlock.

However, over my years as a professional dispute-resolver, I've identified certain patterns of behavior that always increase the chances of successful resolution. For example, there are four words that you can use — in virtually any setting — to disarm your adversary and ensure a more productive conversation.

Those magic words: *Please, help me understand* . . . .

Think, for just a moment, about your last conflict or disagreement. It might've come during a conversation with a colleague on a work project, a misunderstanding with your partner or child about loading the dishwasher, a political debate with a neighbor or Facebook Friend, or a mediation with an adversarial lawyer.

What's your gut reaction when someone challenges your beliefs, disagrees with your assertions, or questions your intellect? We want to fight back. We want to prove our point, show why we're right and they're wrong, and convince the other side of the errors of their ways.

Please, help me understand . . . . Now, these words lead us in a different direction. And I've never seen them fail to advance a negotiation when used tactically and sincerely.

We could have an entire chapter on why, "please, help me understand," is so powerful. For now, though, let's focus on the phrase's usefulness as a builder of humility. Inviting your counterpart to enlighten you opens up constructive dialogue, sets a cooperative tone and displays deference and respect to the other person, and recognizes that you *know that you don't know* everything about what it might take to successfully resolve your differences.

Here's another technique that's steeped in humility: *Ask a question, even when you think you have the answer.* You might find out something you didn't know, or perhaps confirm something you did. At the same time, you give the other person a chance to be heard and the satisfaction of knowing you're paying attention and listening.

Showing you're humble opens the door for you to be more persuasive to the other party. Humility leads to listening, one of the absolutely most effective negotiation tools.

It also creates a sense of reciprocity, which gives your counterpart incentive to then listen to you and be open to your influence and persuasion.

Answers in the Form of Questions

"There is no such thing as a dumb question," as conventional wisdom goes.

You've surely heard this before, probably many times. Teachers, professors, and lecturers of many varieties like to use this phrase, I've found, to encourage discussion. They often want their audience to feel comfortable to voice any misunderstandings, uncertainties, or doubts and encourage them — particularly in group settings — by preemptively indicating that nothing they ask will be viewed as too silly, inconsequential or, well . . . dumb.

Look, I like the sentiment here. I think it's important to create learning environments in which questions are encouraged and not stifled. In doing so, yes, it can be helpful to assure would-be questioners that they can ask whatever they'd like without fear of judgment from their peers or instructors.

But today, let's not pretend there are no dumb questions. Instead, let's redefine and *embrace* them. To make my premise easier to entertain, let's call these "beginner" questions.

Where To Begin?

Beginner questions are highly useful tools that help you elicit information, build rapport, control the flow of conversation, cool emotional responses, and trigger reciprocal humility and rational thinking. For these reasons, effective negotiators and problem-solvers integrate beginner questions into their dispute resolution approaches and habits.

And the best part? Beginner questions (as the name suggests) are easy to use, and they're highly effective in enhancing constructive conversations and negotiations.

Let's start with examples of beginner questions:

- Will you repeat that, please?

- Please, can you help me understand?

- Let's go back to the basics. Can we start over?

- So it sounds like you're saying [*whatever you think the person has said*]. What am I missing?

- What would you do in my shoes?

- I'm not sure I follow you. What do you mean when you say [*a word or phrase the person has used that you aren't sure you (or perhaps even the other person) fully understands*]?

You can work beginner questions like these — just some ideas to get you started — into virtually any discussion. Even if you're in the middle of a disagreement, or you're trying to persuade another person to see things your way — when you have an opportunity to discuss and attempt to resolve your differences — these questions can be worth their weight in gold.

When you test out the "beginner question" approach, you'll experiment and find out how they influence your conversations. The more you use these questions, the easier it will be to incorporate them into your everyday problem-solving patterns. And you'll see how well they work.

Making Your Questions Count

In the meantime, here are a few observations and tips you might find helpful:

- To use beginner questions most effectively and naturally, it truly helps if you're humble. You must be confident enough to acknowledge or imply you don't understand something — and, okay, this could be an initial challenge for some of us. Once over that humility hurdle, though, you can put these types of questions to work for you ASAP.

- The most obvious effect of asking a beginner question? You'll elicit valuable information, of course! Provided you're listening to the answers to your questions, you can clear up misunderstandings, summarize pertinent information, and clarify the other person's position through basic questioning.

- Asking beginner questions, posed skillfully, is a frictionless way to kickstart a conversation. People are often eager to talk about themselves and share their thoughts on a disputed discussion topic. Creating these opportunities helps build rapport, which promotes productive conversation. One straightforward way to give other people the floor, and let them know you value their perspective, is to ask beginner questions. Be patient. I'll frequently give my counterpart what might commonly be viewed as a "softball" question — just a light, easy toss for them to take a big swing at and talk to their hearts' content — even if I almost certainly already know the answer. What's the harm? At worst, the other person gains the satisfaction of fully expressing her position; at best, I also learn something new and gain information that helps us both view our situation more accurately.

- Asking beginner questions helps you control the flow and pace of your conversation. Suppose your counterpart starts to become emotional in a way you feel might turn the discussion in an unproductive direction. Or say you want to guide your drifting conversation back to a topic you deem a priority. Work in a beginner question to get things on track. Refocusing on objective elements of your conflict can help you recover common ground and shift towards verifiable facts. Or perhaps you'd like a moment to consider something that's been said and need time to process and respond. Maybe you want to slow the pace of the discussion. Beginner questions can help here, too.

- I've found that you can use beginner questions to help the other person see *their own position* more clearly. Inviting your counterpart to explain the opposing view will, in some cases, bring dubious claims or fuzzy thinking to the surface when the person actually has to formulate and verbalize that view. Merely speaking the words aloud, in some cases, enables the person to see the discussion more objectively and then, in turn, provides you a reciprocal opportunity to state your views to a more receptive audience.

So, yes, there certainly *are* beginner questions, and even experts can put them to use. These questions do not need to be complicated and, in fact, can be deceptively simple. Embrace beginner questions, experiment with them at home and at work, and see how they can lead you through challenging conversations.

The Power of Silence

Draw on the power of silence. You can try this one not just in a formal negotiation setting, but also at home with your kids, spouse or partner, at work, at school, or in any discussion.

Silence can be a powerful tool for many reasons. One of the most critical – and deceptively simple – is that it gives us a chance to listen to what the other person is saying. I mean, actually LISTEN. Leaving some air space after your counterpart speaks lets you process what's being said without feeling a need to push back immediately.

When someone else is talking, do you find yourself thinking about what you'll say next before the other person is finished? True listening is crucial but can be challenging; periods of silence make it easier.

And you'll find, too, that when you're comfortable allowing for strategic silence in your discussion, your counterpart will be tempted to fill the void and continue speaking. Most people are bothered by a conversation pause and will face an instinctive urge to talk during a break of even a second or two. So go with it. Let them talk. *Listen.*

The more the other person speaks, too, the more he or she can "vent." You might be surprised how moving past that verbal and emotional venting will then allow you to:

- learn from what the other side is saying;

- make the other person more comfortable and feel he or she is being heard; and then

- use that information and person's comfort level to refocus on more productive discourse.

Often – and this can be counter-intuitive – the less a person speaks, the more control and power that person gains in a discussion.

So embrace the silence. It will be tempting to deliver counter-jabs and speak when the conversation lulls, especially during heated moments. However, if you can resist, and if you truly commit to listening and understanding what the other side is saying, the more effective you'll be in harnessing the power of silence and ultimately resolving your differences.

More on Dunning-Kruger and Illusory Superiority

At a critical juncture during a mediation last week, each party announced abruptly that its position was firm and politely threatened to conclude the negotiation session. They wanted to "take it to the judge" instead of continuing a mediated effort to settle their legal case.

I know, I thought to myself, *I'll help these parties "reality-test" their positions. If I can enable them to see that taking this case to trial is very risky, they'll more appreciate the reality of the situation and value of resolution.*

How Do You Like Your Odds?

In consecutive private caucuses — that is, talking in turn with each party in private — I asked the two experienced, opposing attorneys this question: "So where do you put your odds of winning this case?"

Attorney #1: "We have a 75% chance of winning. Maybe more."

Then, Attorney #2: "I love our position. I'd say 75%. And that's being conservative."

And this happens all the time. In fact, I'm surprised when something like this *doesn't* happen, in some form, during a mediation.

But why? Overestimating our abilities is a most basic human bias, and we are influenced by cognitive "tricks" that make it harder to view situations objectively.

Have you ever been in an argument when both you and the other person — with an opposite view — were *100% certain* that you were right about a fact and the other person was *absolutely, positively wrong*? In the end, (at least) one of you had to be wrong, no? According to a recent study of the American Automobile Association (AAA), nearly 3/4 of American drivers consider themselves to be above-average, and 80% of men say their driving skills are better than average.

I'm no statistician, but I'm pretty sure those numbers don't add up.

Metacognition: As Smart As We Think We Are?

In a nutshell: It's easy to overestimate our abilities, assume we can predict the future better than we can, and seek out evidence to support our arguments and devalue the contradictory.

The Dunning-Kruger effect posits, generally speaking, that because it is so difficult for people to evaluate themselves objectively, we tend to overestimate our competence and underestimate our incompetence. Cornell psychologists Dunning and Kruger examined how a lack of metacognition, or inability to take an objective view of ourselves, can make it exceedingly easy — for those competent and also those relatively incompetent in a given arena — to slip into overconfidence and illusions of superiority.

I fully expect attorneys to be confident in their abilities to win cases in court, and confidence in one's legal skills is surely a good thing. However, there's so much out of our control that goes into whether a case is won or lost. I can't tell you how many times I've seen the "perfect lawsuit" go before a judge, or a panel of judges, and come out in way — based on law, facts, or both — unpleasantly surprising to at least one party to the case.

Two great lawyers might go into a case each thinking they

have a slam-dunk, but they can't both be right in the end. Just like 80% of drivers can't all be all be above average, is it possible that you've overestimated your chance of success in winning a case or being "right" in a dispute?

Try to make it a habit to question your assumptions and consider the other side of your discussion or conflict. It's tough to do, and sometimes you might need a neutral, third party to help, but it pays to beware of the mental traps that can cloud our best judgement.

Winning Negotiations with Humility

The other day, I came across an attorney with whom I'd conducted a mediation about six months ago. In those negotiations, the defense had offered this attorney's client a reasonable settlement package, but the plaintiff/client refused to concede any aspect of her case. She insisted on rolling the dice and "taking it to the judge," despite innumerable red flags and warning signs that cast serious doubt on her claims and credibility.

"We lost the case — I imagine you're not surprised — and now the offer on the table has been sliced by 75%," the attorney noted glumly, shaking his head. "My client just refused to believe that the defense could have any valid points. About anything. She was too stubborn and dug-in. And it cost her the best deal she'll ever see on this case. She really blew it."

Stoic philosophers like Marcus Aurelius have imparted wise observations about the virtue of living humbly. It just so happens that humility is an under-the-radar secret weapon of some of the best negotiators I've ever encountered.

Humble negotiators benefit from being open-minded and have a knack for seeing both the strengths and weaknesses of their positions. With humility comes greater objectivity and a more realistic assessment of risks. Recognizing the role luck and pure chance play in our lives, and appreciating that there can exist great value in perspectives that differ from our own, those that negotiate from a place of humility are better equipped to collaborate and make prudent decisions than those who lack empathy and fail to acknowledge the uncontrollable.

I've observed these traits over the years, but only recently have I been able to pinpoint humility as a root of these negotiators' successes.

Increasingly, cognitive psychologists seem to recognize the impact of humility — and the lack thereof — in any number of contexts. Experts not only know stuff about the world, but they also know the limits of their knowledge and expertise.[10]

Humble people tend to be curious, seeking that elusive objective viewpoint, and more at peace with uncertainty. In my experience, strong negotiators share these traits. They're curious about how their negotiating partners see the world, realize that there are two sides to every coin, and know that we're notoriously inaccurate in our predictions about the future.

We simply don't have the tools to predict as well as we think we can. The humble negotiators understand this, and those who lack humility will find out. Probably when they least expect it.

Beware of Confirmation Bias

The human tendency toward confirmation bias – our inclination to seek out and favor evidence that supports our arguments, and to ignore or devalue contradictory evidence – can lead to damaging errors in judgment at the bargaining table. As a mediator, I see this impact negotiations all the time. Even the most sophisticated attorneys and businesspeople are susceptible, and they can miss key facts or arguments that later come back to bite them in court.

It's easy to become so entrenched in one way of looking at a question that losing perspective is inevitable. Our beliefs skew our neutrality in processing relevant data, and we tend to discount evidence that challenges those beliefs.

And confirmation bias can impact our everyday thinking, as well. Suppose you have a strong opinion on a given issue. What's your view on today's most controversial news story, global crisis, or political debate? Whatever your take, chances are you'll be more likely to seek out, and interpret, information in a manner that supports your position. Social media algorithms and an explosion of accessible online news ensure that justification for your opinion is just a click away. It's in our nature, of course, to like the confirmatory notions we encounter.

It's futile to deny that we are biased in this way – we know it deep down, and academic research backs it up. Rather, let's recognize this most mortal vulnerability, acknowledge competing viewpoints, and scrutinize our positions as if they were not our own. These suggestions apply in professional and personal contexts and help us separate opinion from objective facts.

When weighing a competing viewpoint: Instead of reflexively seeking to prove you're right, consider questioning how you might be wrong. This is no small task, especially when embroiled in a conflict or disagreement, but one essential to sound decision-making and conflict resolution.

Failure to analyze your options and objectively project possible outcomes can lead to miscalculations and assessments of risk. So be wary of the "confirmation bias" trap.

Can You See the Future?

What's In A Forecast?

"Well, they sure got it wrong today. Again! The weather forecasters predicted sunshine, and here we are, soaking wet."

"What was the forecast?"

"They said it was just a 10% chance of rain this afternoon. Ridiculous that we got drenched!"

Have you ever had a conversation like this? I bet you have. "What other job in the world, besides meteorologist, lets you be wrong so often and still remain employed?" you might have asked yourself.

Good question, but hold on a second. Was the forecast wrong?

In the middle of North America's severe storm season, it's common to see weather reports tracking hurricanes and other tropical cyclones. These reports frequently accompany maps showing projected storm paths, often in the forms of forecast cones or "spaghetti models."[11] Using a range of models featuring names like dynamic, numerical, statistical, trajectory, and consensus, teams of meteorologists harness an array of computer technologies and scientific tools to predict the course, timing, and impact of these cyclones.

Have you looked at these maps? On the National Hurricane Center's web site, you can find an example graphic of a 5-day forecast cone. The cone is meant to contain the probable path of a storm center but, if you take a look, you'll note that the path allows for hundreds of miles of potential error. That is, the "cone of uncertainty" is unbelievably wide.[12]

In other words: *We don't really know where this thing is going, but we can analyze available information, generalize, and project.*

A Sure Prediction: Unpredictability

If you're starting to feel comfortable as an armchair meteorologist, then check out the spaghetti plot maps. To us laypersons, the 20+ forecast storm path line graphics seem to crisscross, twist and turn in a jumbled mess, with projections heading in all different directions.

Is the storm heading west, north, or east? Yes . . . no . . . and maybe.

I love studying the weather maps, and I'm amazed how much progress weather-predictive technology has made during my lifetime alone. Still, with all of the available data and professionals to interpret it, precise projection of storms and weather remains out of reach.

Although the limits of weather prediction make forecasters easy targets for skeptics – like your friend who happened to get drenched by a passing thunderstorm – consider that we're all wandering through life like the forecasters. We can have a general sense of how the future will unfold, but a lot of what we see we must extrapolate, make our best guesses, and complete our predictive vision.

And our guesses are most likely cobbled together by much flimsier data than what's available to the folks at Weather.com or the National Oceanic and Atmospheric Administration (NOAA).

The Challenge: Making Forward-Looking Decisions

So how is this relevant to negotiation?

One of the greatest obstacles to compromise and agreement is our inability to reckon with life's inherent unpredictability.

When at the beginning of a mediation I ask both sides how they feel about their lawsuit, and they both tell me they have a 90% chance of winning, how can they both be right? What variables are involved in their predictions, and what assumptions are they making that may or may not be accurate? What cognitive biases might be inhibiting each side from viewing its case objectively?

These ideas, of course, come into play during most disagreements and disputes. Negotiation and conflict resolution require us to make present decisions based on what we anticipate in the future. It's certainly less productive to dwell on the past, something over which we have absolutely no control — and therein lies the great challenge. We can want and hope for things to turn out a certain way, and we can impact outcomes by taking or avoiding actions, but there's still so much we can never anticipate. We must look forward.

Further, it's human nature to seek certainty and predictability. It's easier for our brains to process possible outcomes as binary (yes/no, bad/good, rain/sunshine, etc.) than along a spectrum of possibility. Statistics, probabilities, and percentages are tough to grasp in an actionable way, and our incomplete comprehension, in turn, dilutes the quality of our decision-making.

Negotiating In A World Of Uncertainty

Instead of asking ourselves why the weather forecasters — with all of the tools at their disposal — always seem to get it wrong, it might be more useful to embrace that we're *all* operating in a world of incredible variability and uncertainty. It's pretty amazing how much data, technology, science, and psychology can help us make predictions, but the task remains a daunting one — even for the most skilled predictors.

On top of that, a host of cognitive biases conspire to make our analyses that much more difficult.

When you're negotiating, weighing the value of the deal on the table against your future prospects (finding a better agreement, identifying a new negotiating partner, rolling the dice before a jury, etc.), recall the spaghetti models. Think about the squiggly lines and cones of uncertainty. How much more accurate are we than the experts down in the NOAA lab?

I don't have the answers for these questions. But I believe you're better off at least asking them than assuming a false sense of security.

As you enter a negotiation or discussion in which your position depends, in part, on your ability to project the future: How sure are you of your predictions, and do you know what you might be missing?

Can You Believe Your Eyes?

Check out the two parallel lines in the diagram (I'm a writer, not an artist!) above. Now here's your quiz: Which of the two lines is longer?

Once more, look at the lines closely. Is line B longer than line A, or vice versa?

Perhaps you're familiar with this bit of optical hocus-pocus, commonly known as a version of the Müller-Lyer illusion. Here, the arrowheads hinder us from accurately gauging the lines' lengths. That is — you guessed it — the parallel lines are the same, but the orientation of the inward- and outward-pointing arrows create the illusion that line A is longer.

For our purposes, it doesn't really matter why the Müller-Lyer illusion works to trick our brains. What's especially amazing is that, even when you *know* the lines are identical in length — look a third time, if you have to — our brains *still* try to tell us otherwise.

We've talked about unconscious biases and various cognitive errors that we are prone to commit. Among the most familiar of these is perhaps confirmation bias, our tendency to seek out evidence that supports our positions and to ignore that which weakens our arguments.

For negotiators seeking to make quality decisions at the bargaining table, as well as for all of us trying to maximize our everyday decision-making processes, these biases can fool us into making poor choices. That's a problem.

What's *more* of a problem, however, is not recognizing the prevalence of these biases and their capacity to lead us astray. That is, being "blind to our blindness" can lead to a series of cognitive errors and resulting poor decisions.

As sure as humility is the secret weapon of great negotiators, it's much easier to fall into the notorious Dunning-Kruger trap and remain blissfully unknowing of what we don't know. Failing to take an objective, "big picture" view of a situation can lead to overconfidence and illusions of superiority. When that happens, we unconsciously skew data and make decisions based on faulty information-processing.

The Müller-Lyon illusion is a reminder of how easily our brains can trick us. We can't always believe what we see at first glance. Sometimes we have to take out the ruler and measure, despite what our eyes tell us.

Similar things happen in negotiation, conflict resolution, and everyday decision-making settings, as well. Just like our eyes can be lulled by the directional arrowheads' illusory optical effects, our minds can be deceived by any number of data-processing errors. Whether we see things as we want to see them, over- or underestimate probabilities of future events, or commit any of a range of mental miscues, it's critical to be aware of these tendencies.

The valuable lesson here: We're apt to be fooled, even when we know the lines are the same length. So reevaluate, take the time you need to consider what you see and hear, and check your work.

At the very least, we negotiators can aim to know what we don't know, resist being blind to our blindness, and then strive to make better decisions.

What's in Your Blind Spot?

You've all read those notices on the back of 18-wheel tractor-trailers reminding us, "If you can't see my mirrors, I can't see you." In other words: *Get out of my blind spot!*

Our cars have rearview and sideview mirrors, of course, so we can see what's next to and behind us on the road. Newer cars offer blind spot warning systems, using radar or cameras to monitor the sides and rears of our vehicles and indicate when other cars or objects are near. You might notice a light on your mirror or a "beeping" sound when someone or something lurks close by.

What's the purpose of these blind spot warning systems? Of course, they're there because, even if we adjust our mirrors just so, we can't always visualize absolutely everything around us.

In other words, we all have blind spots. We can't trust everything we see, and we can't rely only upon what we see.

This "blind spot" analogy is relevant in conflict resolution. We all have individual preferences, backgrounds, and cognitive biases that shape our perspectives and opinions. Each of us has a unique life experience and accompanying lens through which to view the world.

To untangle a dispute, it can be helpful to try to understand the other side of the coin. Why? Because, just like our rearview mirror systems, our points of view are susceptible to missing information. Maybe we're not getting the whole picture, or perhaps we can't see it from where we sit. (You see heads, the other person sees tails, and you're both right — you're looking at the same thing, but from opposite sides.)

As a mediator, I spend a lot of time with disputing parties helping them realize they have blind spots. Think of me as those warning lights on the side of your mirrors.

You're saying you'll win in court if this case goes to trial instead of settling, but are you 100% sure of that? Or could you be missing something? Are you seeing the whole picture, or just what your mirrors are showing you? Similarly, what might your counterpart be overlooking that you could highlight or help explain? Can you trip the other person's blind spot warning system?

Mediation — a structured negotiation process — gives parties a deliberate opportunity to turn their heads and actually check their blind spots. You can scan your blind spots in everyday conversations, though, too.

Say you're having a disagreement with a spouse or family member, or with someone at work. *What parts of your position — and the other person's — depend on subjectivity and guesswork? Are you arguing about facts or opinions? What facts might you be missing, and which of your opinions are reasonably debatable?*

There's not always something in your blind spot, but you have to check to be sure. And if something is there, wouldn't you be better off knowing?

PRINCIPLE FIVE: EMPATHY

Top negotiators have a knack for empathizing with their counterparts. Even when they disagree with their adversaries, and whether or not they like their opposing parties at all, these negotiators seem to be able to use empathy – an ability to walk in the shoes of others – to see conflicts from all sides.

When you empathize with someone else, and recognize the other's point of view, the person feels understood. Even more critically, the person feels *you* understand, which helps build rapport between you. And when you've built rapport and expressed empathy, you're setting yourself up to negotiate effectively, resolve conflict, and meet your needs at the bargaining table.

By the way, we're not talking here about *sympathy*, or feeling sorry for someone. Empathy is about at least trying to appreciate where the other person is coming from, what they're really saying and what they need in order to get a deal done. Nor do you need to *love* your negotiating partner; instead, empathy can be a path for you to "help them to help you."

Empathy is a powerful negotiating tool you can use to help get your way, and being empathetic is by no means a weakness. I cannot stress this enough. You can empathize with a person with whom you completely disagree, too. As a matter of fact, to empathize you don't have to feel sorry for — or even like — your counterpart.

Empathy can be a comprehension of how the other person feels, and of the cause for that feeling. Why is this important for a negotiator? So you can ultimately get what you need more effectively.

As is so often the case, negotiation skills that are effective in a conference room or courthouse also work to resolve conflicts in interpersonal relationships. But it takes effort to see a disagreement through the eyes of your spouse, child, parent, sibling, or friend. When you clash with an associate or colleague who clings tightly to an opinion you find irrational or outrageous, it can be difficult to imagine what could possibly possess that person to hold such a belief.

People who are able to empathize, though, can use this superpower to relieve conflicts and manage disputes. Understanding an issue from the other side's perspective helps them to uncover the motivations, main concerns, and overarching needs that must be satisfied to reach an agreement.

Stoics view humanity as part of an interconnected, collective whole, valuing social duty and harmony for the greater good. Epictetus talked about modesty, humility, and the importance of helping others develop their rational nature as an expression of love of humanity. Thus, Stoics consider where words are coming from, not just the words themselves – and, of course, this is the "art of listening" negotiators so frequently emphasize.

Even though you can't expect to control another person's high emotions, you can still help by managing your own responses and at least not fanning the flames on the other side. The "master class" negotiators, though, manage their own emotions and, at the next level, those of other decision-makers. As you try to channel your own emotions towards objective analysis and controlled response, the next-level task would be making it easier for *other* decision-makers to do the same.

Another way to view this: Strip away the non-substantive

issues and distractions – the "noise" – from the essence of what you're trying to accomplish (*i.e.*, your actual deal points). Then see where your true interests overlap for potential mutual gain.

The more you can guide others to, for example, (1) not let their emotions hijack their decision-making, (2) zero in on what they can control, (3) stick to objective points, (4) remain open to new ideas and interpretations, and (5) appreciate your plight, the more you're *winning* as a negotiator.

So how can you activate your empathy superpower to enhance your negotiation skills? Let's look at a few ideas.

First, here's a way you might visualize this empathy concept. Think of it like doing one of those maze puzzles where you need to draw a line that gets from one side of the maze to the goal/target. If you've ever watched your kid do one of these (or maybe you've done this yourself, perhaps some time ago!), you figure out that it's often easier to start from the end and work backwards.

Same with empathy as a negotiation tool. *What does the other person need to get out of this deal, and how can I provide that while still maximizing my part and getting what I need (or my client needs)?*

Always strive to appreciate what's driving your counterpart's behavior, and recognize that all of us – even the seemingly most unsympathetic – are worthy of empathy and compassion. The more you know of the other side, the better you will be able to manage your negotiations and satisfy the needs of both parties to a conflict.

Showing genuine concern for another person, no matter how prickly and gruff an exterior that person might project, can even trigger a surge of *reciprocal* empathy that helps the person understand *your* concerns and viewpoints.

You can lead your counterparts to empathy, too, by asking certain pointed questions. One such question I particularly like to use: *What would you do if you were in my shoes?*

You might be familiar with a flip-flopped version of this

question, which we sometimes use to introduce an offer of advice: "If I were you, I would . . . ." Here, though, instead of you giving an opinion on what action you'd take if you were that other person, you're asking the person to consider *what he or she would do in your place.*

The beauty of this "what would you do?" approach is that it: (1) is simple to execute; (2) shows deference to the other side, which will often engender reciprocal deference and respect; (3) displays your humility in seeking out the other person's advice; (4) gives you an opportunity to better understand your counterpart's thought process; and, finally, (5) subtly forces the other person to consider your perspective.

There are other, more advanced techniques you can use to help your counterpart understand your point of view. For instance:

Invite your counterpart to state *your* position. That's right. Give the other side an opportunity to restate your contention. A simple, straightforward way to do this is to ask the other person to *set forth what he or she believes to be your position.*

If you prefer a more subtle tack, use lines like, "What other questions should I be asking?", "How else should I be thinking about this?", or "Help me understand what I'm missing here."

Bottom line: If you're not empathizing with your negotiating counterpart, you're missing a tremendous opportunity. When you do empathize, you greatly increase your persuasiveness.

During your next conflict or negotiation, listen carefully to the other side, work to understand and recognize their point of view – even if you disagree with and feel no *sympathy* for the opposition – and use empathy strategically to reach your objectives.

Own the Problem, Create the Solution

"That's not my problem."

Whenever a party utters these words at mediation, I know we have some serious work to do as negotiators. The chances of adversaries reaching a consensual agreement remain slim until the players understand that if one party has a problem, everyone has a problem.

"The plaintiff has $100,000 in outstanding medical bills, and what you're offering doesn't cover even half of that."

"*Not my problem*," says defense counsel.

"You're asking the business owner to pay an amount he simply doesn't have. He's already filed for bankruptcy and lost his life savings."

"*That's not our problem*," quips the plaintiff's attorney.

"The injured worker is so angry about being fired and absolutely hates her boss. Her husband is very emotional, too, and they feel completely betrayed."

You guessed it. "*Too bad, but not our problem!*"

"But Daaaaaad. I can't take out the trash because I have too much homework."

"*That's just not my . . .*"

What Is Your Problem, Anyway?

I understand why people say that issues like these aren't

their problems. I really do. If a plaintiff's "feeling betrayed" isn't directly compensable or actionable under the law, why should the defense team care? If your client feels entitled to a certain amount of money at mediation, why should your negotiation be affected by the other side's financial troubles? What does your kid's math homework have to do with the trash going out to the curb, anyway?

In these situations, I try to help people understand that if one party has a problem, *everyone* has a problem around which you must negotiate. More precisely, if one party merely *thinks* it has a problem — even if the other party disagrees and doesn't see it that way — you still have to deal with it if you want to settle your dispute. Anything that potentially stands between you and your goal of settlement, well, becomes squarely your problem. The same is true in less formal negotiations and personal conflicts, too.

Appreciating a problem — a real or perceived challenge or obstacle — from the other party's perspective is a basic exercise in empathy, which itself is a critical element of negotiation mastery. The more you can see an element of the dispute as does your adversary, the better you can design strategies and tactics to move your negotiations closer to agreement. When you are aware of the concerns of the other party, you can then address them through your settlement proposals or otherwise through the mediation process. If you can offer a package that satisfies the other side's primary concerns, then you vastly increase your chances of success.

Here's a simplified example to express the point. Take the emotional employee and his spouse, trying to negotiate a settlement in a workplace injury case. The defense's first response might be along the lines of, "The law doesn't make us pay anything for their frustration, so even if I cared it's simply not our problem."

But if the anger and resentment prevent them from settling the case you want to settle, *isn't it your problem?* Of course it is.

Owning — And Jointly Solving — The Redefined "Problem."

In an actual case I recently mediated, an enlightened defense lawyer recognized that intense emotions on the other side, if not addressed at mediation, would prevent meaningful settlement discussions. Instead of dismissing the frustrations and anger of the decision-makers in the other room, this attorney instead acknowledged them in joint session (a face-to-face, group meeting) through non-confrontational remarks, expressions of understanding, and refocusing on working together towards a constructive resolution.

In this case, ultimately, the parties reached a mediated settlement. And I know for a fact, based on extensive discussions in private caucuses (meeting with the parties separately), that the defense counsel's demeanor and recognition of the parties' joint ownership of potential settlement barriers was a significant factor in the process' success.

The strategic takeaways here, which you can use in a range of negotiation and conflict-resolution settings:

- If any party has, *or even thinks it has*, a problem, then you all have a problem to address before you can reach a satisfactory mutual resolution.

- To influence or persuade — to get someone to act (or not act) in a way you'd prefer — figure out the resistance points and aim to address them. *What's keeping the other players from doing what you'd like, and how can you make it easier for them?* Thinking about the situation from the opposite of your own perspective, for example, helps with this critical part of the resolution process.

- Recognize that one side's obstacle is a shared challenge to own and overcome, collectively, if your goal is mutual agreement.

The People and the Problem

As we've discussed elsewhere, in negotiation settings, focusing on the objective issues in dispute, rather than getting bogged down in personal attacks and one-sided arguments, often leads to effective dialogue. Effective dialogue, in turn, leads to mutual understanding and, ideally, ultimate resolution.

Though discussions grounded in fact and objectivity are preferable to those featuring *ad hominem* insults and baseless critique, negotiation is a quintessentially human exchange. It's always important to understand the other side's perspective in a disagreement, both in your search for "truth" and in order to persuade your counterpart. Even if you're 100% correct about an objective, provable fact, that's not always enough to win an argument or convince someone to see things your way.

Sometimes a conflict's resolution has absolutely nothing to do with substantive issues and everything to do with effectively managing "soft skills" and what might appear to be non-objective details.

It can be tempting to – and you should – come into a mediation or negotiation with hard numbers, financial calculations, and cogent arguments that you think prove an objectively "correct" result. However, remember that how you package your analysis and frame your proposals can also be determinant. Consider:

- Do some people respond better to being asked to do something, as opposed to being told to do it?

- Are you more inclined to cooperate with someone you like, or with someone who's threatened and antagonized you?

- Might some of us respond to a request less favorably, say, on a dreary Monday morning before our first cup of coffee, than we might on a Thursday afternoon before a long holiday weekend?

- Are you more willing to listen to a person who has first taken the time to empathize with and listen to you?

- Can an artful negotiator frame an idea or request in such a way that the other person doesn't even realize a request is being made?

Surely. Absolutely.

Questions like these are endless, and certainly it helps to know the tendencies and preferences of your negotiating partner when devising your approach. As a mediator, I spend a tremendous amount of time guiding parties as to which "packaging" of a proposal might be best received. My suggestions depend on a range of factors dictated by the particular situation and personalities involved in the underlying dispute.

When seeking to resolve a conflict: Be prepared to address the problem, aim for a mutual understanding of any substantive disagreements, and then try to anticipate those nuances — beyond the facts and figures — that matter most to an effective resolution.

"What would you do in my shoes?"

By now you know how important it is to gain an understanding of the other side to an argument, negotiation, or dispute. You don't have to agree with your opponent's position on a matter, but for a number of reasons you'll benefit from at least appreciating where and why you see things differently.

So let's say you're an open-minded, inquisitive, collaborative negotiator whose strategy and tactics are informed by Stoic philosophy and behavioral psychology. That's great! But what if your adversary is stubborn, dug-in, shortsighted, and absolutely convinced that he or she has all the right answers?

Quite frankly, it sounds like you're in a tough spot. However, here's a group of tools you can employ to guide your discussion in a productive direction.

Just as you know it's valuable to see things from the other person's perspective, help the other person to understand your point of view. Realizing that people tend to reactively devalue your point if you try to force it upon them — resisting an idea simply because it comes from an "opponent" — use a different tactic:

Invite your opposition to restate YOUR position. That's right. Give the other side an opportunity to express your contention. A simple, straightforward way to do this is to ask the other person to set forth what he or she believes to be your position. If you prefer a more subtle tack, use questions like, "What would you do if you were in my shoes?", "What other questions should I be asking?", "How else should I be thinking about this?", or "Help me understand what I'm missing here."

Frequently, negotiators can become so focused on their own arguments that they lose objectivity. This mere exercise —

restating your position — will help that other person appreciate not only that there is another side to the argument, but also where your argument has relative strengths. By inviting your negotiating partner to argue your side of an issue, you instantly convey a degree of respect and give yourself an opportunity to listen.

Ideally, this dynamic will create the beginnings of a reciprocal effect that allows the other person to listen when it's your turn to talk. People are more likely to value your thoughts if you show that you value theirs.

Plus, more often than not, this exchange will let you identify gaps in your opponent's understanding of what your position actually is. That, in turn, gives you an opening to clarify misconceptions and then, most importantly, shift toward more constructive problem-solving.

Empathizing With the Enemy

I was recently reminded of a case I mediated last year, one of the most formidable I've ever faced. My goal was to help the plaintiff and defendant reach a consensual, out-of-court settlement that would end their ongoing legal battle.

The mediation was difficult for various reasons, as the plaintiff had suffered a devastating work injury that led to high medical bills, an uncertain future, and a case implicating complex legal issues. The defendant had taken an aggressive stance throughout the case and viewed reasonable settlement values vastly differently than did the plaintiff.

Perhaps the most challenging aspect of the case, though, was the defense attorney. He was tough, hard-nosed, and unwavering in his view of the case and his client's negotiating position. The plaintiff's attorney was unable to make any headway in breaking down the defense, and I, too, felt like I was talking to a brick wall when attempting to help defense counsel see the weaknesses in his case.

As the day wore on, I entered defense counsel's caucus room and caught him on the phone. I started to leave the room, so as not to disturb what I assumed to be a private conversation with the attorney's client, but he gestured me to stay. As I sat down silently, unable to help but note the audible side of the phone conversation, I heard words like "cancer," "scary," and "let's see what the doctor says." I could see the panic on the attorney's face, as he concluded the conversation and ended softly with, "I love you, Dad."

Somewhat taken aback, unprepared for what I had heard and uncertain how to proceed, I asked the defense attorney if everything was okay. He calmly explained that his elderly father was recently diagnosed with cancer and had been awaiting test results. I expressed my sympathy and tried to help him, in some small way, handle the aftermath of the brief conversation. The attorney apologized for the interruption, thanked me for my concern, and insisted he was ready to resume mediating.

As we transitioned back to talking about the mediation, I saw the attorney in a different light. He was still an extremely tough negotiator, and he appeared to be completely unmoved by the accident that was the subject of our case, or by the resulting life-changing injury to the plaintiff. But I still saw him distinctly, now as more of a complete person, and as someone who must have felt more than he was showing. After all, he was a human being, and human beings have feelings and all kinds of stuff they have to deal with in their lives.

Yes, I did feel some sympathy towards the attorney but also, more relevant for negotiations, I had a surge of empathy. I tried to understand more of the attorney's perspective, what might have been causing him to act the way he was during our negotiations, and how I could perhaps build further rapport by giving him the "okay" to be human.

Showing genuine concern for another person, no matter how prickly and gruff an exterior that person might project, can even trigger a surge of reciprocal empathy that helps the person understand the real-life obstacles facing the aggrieved party in the opposite room.

The case ultimately settled, at the conclusion of challenging negotiations, but we can learn a more important lesson here.

Always strive to understand what's driving your counterpart's behavior, and recognize that all of us – even the seemingly most unsympathetic – are worthy of empathy and compassion. The more you know of the other side, the better you will be able to manage your negotiations and satisfy the needs of both parties to a conflict.

Unusually High Call Volumes

"We are experiencing unusually high call volumes. Your call is important to us and will be answered in the order in which it was received. Your current wait time is . . . *43 minutes*."

Cue the elevator music. You're going to be on hold for a while, so you might as well settle in.

Ah, the holidays. A time for good cheer, fellowship . . . and gift returns.

Followers of *The Stoic Negotiator* know that here we observe negotiation through a wide lens. Embracing everyday negotiating opportunities and being on the lookout for non-traditional "negotiation" scenarios we face daily gives us a fresh perspective on the related disciplines of persuasion, influence, and conflict resolution.

Are you engaging with someone else in an effort that requires coordination and cooperation to make a joint decision? Are you seeking to sway another person to see things your way and influence the other's behavior? Do you have a conflict to resolve or manage in a way that helps reach a compromise or optimal result?

Yes, negotiation skills can guide you in any number of situations like these.

So let's return to the "on hold" scene. Suppose you had purchased a holiday gift you needed to return — a shirt that was too small for your child — called the appropriate retailer, and were patiently waiting to speak with a Customer Service Representative ("CSR").

Why did you call? You have a dispute to resolve: You received a shirt that doesn't fit and need to send it back. The seller has been paid and wants to keep a sale; however, the seller also wants to protect its reputation, retain you as a happy customer, and earn your future business.

When you call the CSR, then, are you negotiating? Of course you are.

Especially during the holiday season, being a CSR is tough. After all, the crux of the job entails fielding complaints, managing expectations of disappointed (or worse!) customers, and trying to keep people happy — all while protecting the best interests of your company.

And, let's face it, customers aren't calling CSRs unless they have a problem. So CSRs aren't necessarily dealing with people on their best days and, after sitting through what can be exorbitant holiday-season phone or chat wait times, customers who finally reach a live operator are raring to unload their frustrations.

Of course, as a prospective caller, your preliminary tactical choice is *when* to initiate your call. Timing can be critically important in these situations, and you should be strategic about when to engage a CSR. *What day of the week is it? What time is it? Do you call during the holiday crunch, or can you afford to wait until the heightened stress and most intense pressure of the season subsides? When you ultimately present your problem, what would allow you to leave the conversation and transaction satisfied?*

Speaking of which, what *are* your goals for the call? And what's your strategy (do you have one?) for getting there? You'll enter the conversation with, ideally, a range of acceptable outcomes, and you'd aim as high as reasonably possible. You have many variables to consider as you approach this type of — yes — negotiation.

Today, though, let's flip the script. Consider *what CSRs can do* to make these calls most effective.

You know the difference between a useful CSR and an ineffective one. We've all experienced it. *So what are some basic negotiation skills CSRs can utilize to make us feel better and sense that our situation is managed appropriately? And what can we learn about effective negotiation from these interactions?*

- **Listening**. The first thing I want to know when I call a CSR is that someone is actually listening. We're justifiably skeptical after being placed in an automated phone queue and listening to generic jazz loops for 43 minutes. It's essential that a CSR give callers the sense that they are important (beyond the recording telling us "your call is important," etc., etc.), the company values the customer's concerns, and that someone in the organization will take time to listen and make things right.

- **Acknowledging**. When a CSR acknowledges a customer's issue, that provides the customer a feeling of being validated and recognized. During one of the most effective CSR calls in recent memory, the CSR clarified, repeated, and restated my complaint better than I could have put it myself. This gentleman took the time necessary to unpack my issue and skillfully presented it back to me in a way that reflected his complete understanding. Not surprisingly, hearing the restatement helped me see the issues objectively and began to open my mind to the CSR's perspectives.

- **Questioning**. The most effective CSRs ask thoughtful questions as part of their intake process. Asking questions, particularly of the open-ended variety, is important for several reasons: (1) helping the CSR fully understand the situation; (2) providing the caller an opportunity to express any and all issues; (3) allowing the caller space, if necessary, to vent frustrations, and feel sufficiently heard, before turning towards possible solutions; and (4) conveying a message of concern and desire to solve the problem. Many of these calls, too, end with a catch-all question: "Is there any other way in which I can be of assistance today?" This allows callers parting opportunities to empty the tank and share whatever else might be on their minds.

- **Empathy**. "I'm really sorry about this, and it must be frustrating. We'll do everything we can to resolve your issue." It is extremely valuable for a CSR to be able to empathize with the caller and express that over the phone. Even if the customer and the CSR are strangers meeting for the first time on their call, the mere act of displaying empathy can go a long way towards putting the caller at ease and lessening frustration associated with the situation.

- **Emotions**. As hopping mad as a caller might be, an effective CSR simply won't react with anger or anything close to a temper. As a company delegate, you just can't do that and, what's more, coming from an emotional place is not generally a productive means of negotiating. Instead, effective dispute resolvers know that we always have the choice of how to respond to conflict. Besides managing their own responses and modeling calm conversation, the best CSRs help callers pause and even redirect their emotions, guiding them to a rational, more objective place. This frequently leads discussion towards a mutually satisfactory solution.

At the end of the day, we want results and our complaints resolved. That's true. But often our perceptions of situations and proposed solutions depend on our state of mind — and that's directly related to negotiation skills.

After your next call, think about what your CSRs do that

works well — and what not so well — to resolve disputes. *Which of their techniques will you use when negotiating elsewhere in your everyday life?*

---

[1] Frankl, Viktor E., *Man's Search for Meaning: An Introduction to Logotherapy*. Boston: Beacon Press, 1962.

[2] Fisher, Roger, et al., *Getting to Yes: Negotiating Agreement Without Giving In*, 3rd ed. New York: Penguin Books, 2011. Perennial best-seller *Getting to Yes* describes the "principled negotiation" method that came out of the *Harvard Negotiation Project* (*see* https://www.pon.harvard.edu/tag/the-harvard-negotiation-project/). This book is must-read material for those looking to learn more about modern negotiation theory.

[3] The Socratic method involves a "questioning" persuasion technique, pioneered by a Greek philosopher – a precursor to the Stoics – named, of course, Socrates. Socrates used this question-and-answer tool, sure to strike fear in the hearts of law students everywhere, to raise doubt in a speaker's mind as to whether what was thought to be known was actually known. *The Stoic Negotiator*™ has explored this method elsewhere, and for more you can start here.

[4] Witten, Douglas J., *Mediation Essentials Toolkit: A Practitioner's Emergency Survival Guide* (2021) is available in digital and paperback editions.

[5] *See, e.g.*, Stanovich, K. E., West, R. F., & Toplak, M. E. (2013), Myside Bias, Rational Thinking, and Intelligence, *Current Directions in Psychological Science*, 22(4), 259–264.

[6] "Reactive devaluation," a concept addressed elsewhere in this compilation, is a recurring *The Stoic Negotiator*™ topic. It's also a favorite of mediators and strongly supports enlisting the aid of neutral, objective, negotiation and conflict resolution guidance.

[7] Kahneman, Daniel, *Thinking, Fast and Slow*. New York: Farrar, Straus and Giroux, 2011.

[8] *See* Kahneman, D., & Tversky, A. (1979), Prospect Theory: An Analysis of Decision Under Risk, *Econometrica*, 47, 263-291.

[9] What's more, 80% of U.S. male drivers consider themselves above average. For more on the underlying AAA study, *see* https://newsroom.aaa.com/2018/01/americans-willing-ride-fully-self-driving-cars/.

[10] Nobel Prize-winning psychologist and economist Daniel Kahneman has even referred to overconfidence (that is, the opposite of humility) as the most damaging of our decision-making flaws, and the one he'd most like to eliminate if he could. *See* https://www.theguardian.com/books/2015/jul/18/daniel-kahneman-books-interview.

[11] Some of these models, maps, and trackers are truly amazing. For instance, take a look at these overviews from the National Oceanic and Atmospheric Administration (NOAA): https://www.nhc.noaa.gov/modelsummary.shtml; and https://www.nhc.noaa.gov/aboutcone.shtml.

[12] Weather.com also has useful information on "cones of uncertainty" (https://weather.com/science/weather-explainers/news/tropical-storm-cyclone-forecast-cone-hurricane) and the infamous hurricane "spaghetti models" (https://weather.com/science/weather-explainers/news/spaghetti-models-tropics-tropical-storm-hurricane).

ABOUT THE AUTHOR

Douglas J. Witten

Douglas J. Witten, Esq., principal of Innovative ADR International LLC, is an attorney, mediator, arbitrator, and negotiation coach who has 28+ years of professional experience. He has assisted parties resolve legal disputes in 1400+ cases and offers private dispute resolution services, in English and Spanish, across areas including healthcare, workplace injuries, and commercial matters.

Doug has written and presented extensively on legal, healthcare, negotiation, mediation, and dispute resolution topics. His other publications include The Stoic Negotiator™ newsletter (stoicnegotiator.substack.com) and Mediation Essentials Toolkit: A Practitioner's Emergency Survival Guide (https://www.amazon.com/Mediation-Essentials-Toolkit-Practitioners-Emergency-ebook/dp/B08WRJPXMN).

Doug earned a B.B.A. from Emory University Goizueta Business School, a J.D. from New York University School of Law, and an LL.M. from the University of Houston.

BOOKS BY THIS AUTHOR

Mediation Essentials Toolkit: A Practitioner's Emergency Survival Guide

The Mediation Essentials Toolkit: A Practitioner's Emergency Survival Guide is designed for the legal practitioner seeking usable techniques to enhance mediation tactical advocacy skills. Attorneys and legal professionals who advocate on behalf of their clients at mediation can draw on the tools this handbook outlines to improve negotiation tactics, train associates on the basics of mediation practice, build trust among fellow lawyers and clients, and generate long-term, positive results. The Mediation Essentials Toolkit is concise and easy to read. This handbook is written for the busy professional looking for time-tested guidance on how to survive, and thrive, at the negotiating table even when the odds weigh against success. Every case is unique, and each negotiation has its own composition and flavor. Sometimes, the facts of your case are bad and the law is against you. Other times, you have either good facts or good law, but not both. However, if you incorporate the described mediation tools into your legal practice, to whatever degree, you can help your clients optimize their negotiation satisfaction over the long haul.

www.ingramcontent.com/pod-product-compliance
Lightning Source LLC
Chambersburg PA
CBHW071208240526
45470CB00018B/1594